Court Quest

COURT QUEST

Playing Women's Squash
in the USA and Canada 1992-1994

Joy Conrad

Bench Press Books
Kamloops, British Columbia, Canada

Court Quest
Playing Women's Squash in the USA and Canada 1992-1994
by Joy Conrad

Bench Press Books
PO Box 453
Kamloops, British Columbia, V2C 5L2, Canada
Toll-Free: 1-800-573-5779
Fax: 1-250-314-6232
Email: info@benchpressbooks.com
Website: www.benchpressbooks.com

Copyright© 2002 by Joy Conrad
All rights reserved. Except for reviews, no part of this book may be reproduced in any manner or form without permission from the publisher.

Cover design concept and logo by Dave Somerville.
Interior and cover design by Carol Creasy of Little Cottage Graphics.

Printed and bound by:
iPoDs - Interior Print On Demand Services, Winfield, B.C., Canada

National Library of Canada Cataloguing in Publication Data
Conrad, Joy, 1943-
Court Quest: Playing Women's Squash in the USA and Canada 1992-1994

Includes glossary
ISBN #0-9730297-0-6

1. Conrad, Joy, 1943- 2. Squash players—Canada—Biography. 3. Women squash players—Canada—Biography. 4. Squash rackets (Game)—Tournaments. I. Title
GV1003.62.C66A3 2002   796.343'092   C2002-910653-2

The publisher acknowledges Enid Rice Conrad and W. "Con" Conrad for financial and moral support.

Some characters and events in this account were fictionalized to protect individual privacy and identity.

DEDICATION

This story is dedicated to squash players everywhere, as well as those who don't play or can't play anymore, but nevertheless, love the sport of squash racquets.

Let us appreciate bodies that work well, minds that play, personalities that make much happen, and spirits that soar on the court, even though sometimes off the court they don't.

May We Drop Until We Drop

Court Quest

The International Squash Court

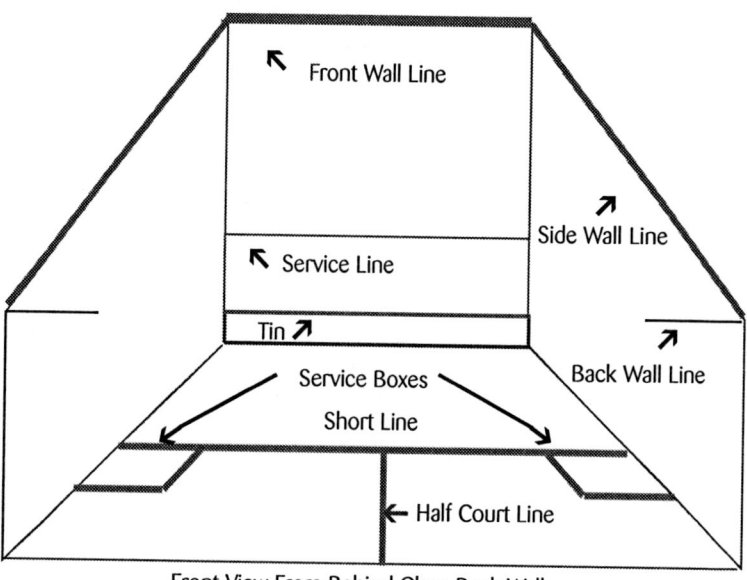

Front View From Behind Glass Back Wall

Contents

First Efforts	9
Ceremony	10
Jericho Vets and Masters Tournament	13
Tamara's Hope	17
Challenge Court	18
Competitive Spirit	20
Lightening and Lead	22
Men's Draw	26
Mark Talbott Exhibition	30
Training Pay-off	31
Women's Squash Program	31
Skill and Cunning Vets Tournament	34
Puget Sound Tournament	38
Ambivalence	42
Decision	44
Gloom	47
Bouncing Back	50
Inspiration	51
Playing Men	52
Adjustments	54
A Quickie Tournament	54
Summer Wonderings	56
Feeling Sorry for Myself	59
A New Season	60
Doing It	62
Training Tough	63
Cedar Hills Vets Tournament	64
Arbutus Vets Tournament	71
Age, Sport Bras, Head Bands, and Kids	76
A Little Lesson	78
Competitive Dynamics	79
The Nutritionist	80
Which Tournament and When?	81
More Training	83

Court Quest

Crisis	85
Doldrums	86
A Lift	90
Something Beckoning	92
West Coast Vets Tournament	94
Preparing	99
Dreary Days	100
Skill and Cunning Vets Tournament	103
Tamara Trying	107
Ethereal Effects	108
Women's Weekend Tournament	112
Loss, Infatuation, and Decision	119
The Vetter the Better Tournament	122
Deciding for Lessons	126
Ranking In British Columbia	129
The Seattle City Championships	130
Now What?	131
Taking Action	132
More Hurdles	136
Hurdles and Hope	140
United States National Softball Squash Championships	142
Afterward: The Real Change of Life	158
Glossary	159
Acknowledgements	163
Colophon	164
Quick Order Form	165

First Efforts

At six in the morning I show up for my regular Masters swim workout at my athletic club.

"OK, Joy, you finished with warm-up? Today I want you to do 10 times 2 for speed," says the swim coach.

"I don't think I can. I barely made it here."

"A cold?"

"Yeah, not bad though. Just enough to drop me down."

The swim coach looks at the roll of Life Savers I have placed on the pool deck above my lane. "What are the Life Savers for?"

"In case I cough."

"Huh, OK. Then just continue like it's a long warm-up and do 50 lengths or get out when you feel like it."

"OK, I'll try." I swim slowly and methodically, checking my breathing, noticing how hard it is to breathe deeply. *"Stop it, don't be afraid, you're not going to hyperventilate! Take it easy."*

That afternoon I play squash with Tamara.

"Ho ho, good get! What's the score?" I ask.

"Eight—four. Serving right."

We play a rally and clash at the T.

"Let, please."

"OK. Good call."

"Eight—four."

I should run for the ball, but don't. Tamara gets the point and the game. We walk off the court.

"I've had enough. I think I'm going home now. Don't feel—"

"Sounds like you've got a cold."

I nod and head to the women's locker room with my squash bag and racquet.

That evening I cough while cuddling with Rob. "So you don't think you're training too much?"

"No, I've got to. It's just my silly fears about getting sick and dying from Muppet Pneumonia like my colleague at work. She wasn't even old and decrepit!"

"Not again, Joy, your imagination. The gunk you cough up turns slightly green and you think you've got Jim Henson Muppet Pneumonia."

"You know, people who swim, have asthma, and have to use those whiffers? I don't know how they do it. That'd be so scary."

"Now you've got asthma, too. And of course you've got lung cancer, too." His is a gentle mocking.

"OK, I get your drift. You always say the right thing to pull me out of these exaggerations. What if I can't sustain this pace of training? What if I can't get to the point where I can play three five game matches in a day-and-a-half, like you have to in serious competition?"

"Then you'll just have to beat 'em in four game matches. Let's go for a roll in the hay."

Ceremony

The women of my book group are sitting around the living room, some on sofas and chairs, some on pillows. We are all peri-menopausal, menopausal, or post-menopausal. We like to read books and talk about them after a potluck dinner. This night is different. A tall, somber, gentle-voiced woman is speaking over background guitar music.

"This evening's ceremony has been designed with an awareness of our mothers, grandmothers, and great-grand-mothers who, in earlier times, were inhibited from marking their own mid-life passage—their release from the physical tasks of childbearing and child-raising, the cessation of menstruation, finally giving in to their personal creativity without the distractions and responsibilities of maintaining their family."

"We hope to convey a positive tenor to this life cycle event which is still feared and misunderstood by so many women and men even in today's enlightened society. We are here to clarify our gender identity, so often blurred by society at this time in our lives. We are here to acknowledge and celebrate our transitional state. We intend to understand and recognize the meaning of mid-life for women who have experienced it, are experiencing it now, or will soon enter its phases."

"At mid-life the drive, the creative impulse is still there surging forward. We can nurture our creative life long after our children are gone from the nest, and we can direct our energies and talents toward projects that need tending in the larger community. The world needs the wisdom, the experience, the talents, the humor of its women."

"Please share your visions for the future—your future. Tell us how you are incorporating into your life what you have learned is right for you. Tell us your passion."

One by one we stand and speak, Talking Stick in hand. When we finish, we pass the Talking Stick to the next speaker. When I get it, I stand and look intently at the group seated before me. Holding my squash racquet in one hand and the Stick in the other, I begin to speak. (I am wearing a floor length midnight blue silk dress embroidered with gold thread, a gift from one of my Egyptian students, and I feel exquisite.)

"I have had a good life. I grew up in a stable family. The main message was be excellent in all you do. On the one hand, I heard be a wife and mother, the most honored roles for a woman. On the other hand, I heard be educated, be a career woman, go out to adventure. So of course, I tried to do both. I got educated, began to teach at a college, and then heard the click of feminism. I began to see the world differently, but this didn't stop me from falling in love. I became a lover, an almost-wife, and a mother. As the years passed, I did sports as much as I could—tennis, swimming, skiing, softball, ping-pong, and running. I continued to teach and became a leader of an influential feminist group.

At the age of 28, the age of motherhood, I discovered squash. I began to fit an hour of squash playing into my daily schedule as balance to full-time mothering. I began to get good at squash. I played and played and began to compete. I got much better. I began to teach squash and help put on tournaments.

Then I got diverted from squash. For about ten years while my son was in middle school and high school, I got into competitive swimming—not my own, but my son's. I became a swimming mother, driving to early morning workouts, after school workouts, and weekend swim meets.

After my son went off to university, I got back into squash. Alas, I was no longer young. No matter. I would try anyway. This is where I am today—trying anyway. I am training to become as good as I can get at my age. I play a lot, do fitness classes, and cross train. My goal is to go to the U. S. Nationals and play very well in my age group—which will be 50-55 at the next Nationals. I love squash, love hitting the ball, and love the strategy of it. I promise to train hard for a year or two, get to Nationals, and then come back here to you, so we can celebrate together."

As I speak, I sense the light in the room and the rapt

attention of the women. I feel full of willingness, enthusiasm, optimism, and approval. As I sit down, still gripping my squash racquet tightly, I sense something inside me being solidified.

Jericho Vets and Masters Tournament
Jericho Squash and Tennis Club
Vancouver, British Columbia, Canada

I say goodbye to Rob by telephone. He will not be going with me. He never goes with me. He is leading a double life that doesn't include going on trips with me. As much as I love him there is something major missing in my life. I am living a double life, too. Although my dedication to him is sincere, I am always vaguely on the lookout for someone else.

So I pack my suitcase, making sure to include my dancing shoes and dancing dress. I double-check the strings on my squash racquet and I begin my drive north from Seattle towards Canada.

At the United States-Canada border I tell a customs officer that I am on my way to play in a squash competition and am planning to stay the weekend. He smiles slightly.

At the Jericho Squash and Tennis Club near Point Grey in Vancouver, I check in. On a squash court I warm-up.

Later, I look around at who is there and recognize no one. I keep my eyes open for attractive men, a habit I have gotten into.

It is time to play my first match. I am playing level B, the skill level third from the top, the other levels being A and Open. Many of the B women are over 40. I focus strongly and win.

Court Quest

In the club restaurant after my shower I put my racquet and sport bag on the floor next to an empty table. My peripheral vision senses greetings from the next table. A good-looking squash player is sitting there with three others. He invites me to join them. I acknowledge him and start towards their table. He smiles and introduces himself as Jack. I am unsure of where to sit. As the two women open up a space for my chair between them, I introduce myself and meet Mona and Don Gunn as well as Jack's friend, Bev.

We women chat as the men order drinks and ask about the food. "So, Mona, do you play squash?" I ask.

"No, I don't. I'm into softball."

"Softball–not softball squash?"

"Slow–pitch softball, for twenty years, women's league."

"Oh. And Bev, how about you? Do you play squash? What do you play?"

"Well, I've never been much for sports. Jack is teaching me to ski. He bought me some skis and boots."

Mona looks at Bev with acceptance. Mona and Don have been Jack's squash buddies for twenty years. Whatever he wants is what they want.

I cannot help my thoughts: *"Such a traditional thing to do– younger woman takes up what her new man wants her to take up. Where is your independence, lady? Oh, Jack, why did you bring her?"*

Jack watches us women. He peers at me and thinks, *"My God, I'm so attracted to you, why didn't I come alone?"*

I sense his interest in me and hold it within my instinctual self.

The next day I play my second match and win, but not easily. Jack plays a match, but is erratic and loses. I see his scores on the draw sheet. *"I could have predicted a loss, Jack. You're trying to do too much at once."*

During the day I avoid Jack as much as possible, although I can't get out of refereeing a match with him. We keep our tensions subterranean.

On the beach I walk by myself, review my matches so far, plan my next match and psyche myself up. While nibbling on a Power Bar, I lapse into fantasies of dancing with Jack. *He is a splendid dancer and twirls me around and around. Abruptly flashes of dancing with Rob bombard my fantasy. Dancing at a party is how Rob and I met years ago. Though he was not and still is not a fine dancer, his presence as he held me enveloped me thoroughly, and it was, as they say, attraction at first sight.*

That evening I play my third match. I focus well but am outplayed by a better player, Mariza Ohlssen. Mariza is from a rival club in Seattle and is two months older than me. We will be in the same age group forever. Mariza is quick, strong, and ardently competitive. She is an unexpected obstacle to my goal of doing really well in my age group at Nationals, whatever year I make it there. *"My nemesis, already I have met my nemesis. How will I ever get by her?"*

Early Saturday evening near the registration area, I stand dressed for traveling. While looking at photos of previous tournaments, I sense Jack beside me as he nudges me slightly. Startled, I jump away. Not acknowledging discomfort, we look through the photos together.

"Will you be going to the dinner-dance tonight, Joy?"

"No, Jack, I decided not to. I lost. I don't play tomorrow."

"That's too bad. I bet you're a terrific dancer."

I scrutinize him. "As a matter of fact, I am. Are you?"

"Oh, I do all right. I like to dance the night out here and then go to a club and dance some more, until I'm really exhausted."

We part and I record this information in my mind. I yearn to dance well into a night—with him or anyone. I don't care about Jack at this point; I simply miss dancing. Rob and I have our routine and it doesn't include dancing anymore.

As I move to exit the club, Jack whispers, "Farewell, I'll call you and come to Seattle for a tournament. I can get your number from the squash association." He squeezes my hand. I smile and register ambivalence.

In my car going towards the U. S. border, I remember the good and the sloppy parts of my matches. Again my mind lapses into a dancing fantasy with Jack. Then I am disturbed by a flash-forward to Rob. I am certain he is sitting quietly at his desk in his office at the university, correcting papers, waiting for me to return.

When I arrive, I call him and he comes over. We talk and make love and sleep.

The next day, even though I feel discouraged, I buckle down to more training. At this time I cannot see how I can get good enough to beat Mariza. If I can never get good enough, then I don't deserve to go to U. S. Nationals. *"What I can do, as usual, is give it my best try."*

A sensation of fierce determination enters my spirit and after some moments, conceals itself.

Tamara's Hope

Tamara and I are hitting, wearing old duds, and getting on with the day. I serve a lob. Tamara hits the tin. Side out. Serving left, I hit a side-arm serve. Tamara returns it weakly down the alley. I run forward and drop it short for a winner. Soon the score is 5-0 mine. Tamara mutters to herself, *"Come on, Tamara. Concentrate."* I stay silent as we hit some more. Tamara continues to hit tin or above the out line. I get three more points.

It is 3-8, Tamara serving and she serves out. Side out. I serve. Tamara jumps up to volley the ball. The ball careens onto the ceiling and down. End of game. We walk off the court and sit down, toweling off a bit.

"I'm sorry. Joy. I don't know what's the matter with me. You know I usually get right in there."

"I imagine what's going on. You and your husband made love last night and you're nervous about playing too hard because you don't want—you want to make the best possible chance for conception."

Tamara does not look embarrassed "It's interesting that you say that. It is on my mind. My temperature is right. There's so much stress in my life right now."

"Sometimes I can tell by the way a woman plays, that she's having her period. As I get closer to the time when I won't be subjected to that instability, I wonder if I'll actually play better."

"My husband doesn't really want—he's happy with our four-year-old son. But you know, Joy, I think if I don't try now, I'll regret it later."

"How old are you exactly?"

"Forty-two. I look it, don't I?"

"Nah. But the stress. I understand about stress. I

wanted another one in my 40's, too, but the—come on, let's play another game before we get chilled."

We move onto the court and play again but it doesn't flow and we quit.

Challenge Court

Later at the Challenge Court I see Terry Koss, the unofficial squash guru at our club, one of the few men who play with women, a nice guy all around.

"Hi, Terry. How are you?"

"Hi, Joy."

"How does this Challenge Court work?"

"You sign your name on the paper and wait until it's your turn to play a game. The winner stays on."

"Thanks. Are you playing today?"

"Yeah, with Bill. On Court Two."

"Not the Challenge Court?"

"No, those guys are—I like to play at least three games in a row. I really need to play hard after a long day at work."

"Oh."

I sit down, racquet in hand, and watch two men play hard, fast, and intensely. They have long rallies. As they come off the court, the winner acknowledges me and gestures me onto the court.

I enter the court only to be dismayed by puddles of sweat on the floor. I retreat to get some towels and start to wipe up the sweaty water. Then I stop. I leave the towels soaking up water and move to the other side of the court. I start to hit rail shots to myself. As my opponent comes onto the court, I introduce myself and we shake hands. Then I gesture to the water.

Challenge Court

"Uh, would you like to wipe up your sweat?"

The player shows surprise and looks at me in puzzlement.

"Or is it Harry's?"

"Yeah, Harry sweats."

Giving up, I push the towels off the court with my foot, shut the glass door, and return to the court.

In deference, the guy tosses me the ball and says, "Here, go ahead and serve."

"OK."

What happens is fast action: short rallies, quickly hit balls, valiant efforts by me, and complete control of the game by him. After he has proven his dominance, he eases up, loses a little focus, and loses some points. I change from mediocre playing—slow and bad—to much better with some winning shots. At the end of the game, which the guy wins easily, we shake hands, and leave the court.

The men hanging around the Challenge Court appear restless and chatter among themselves. The next guy up goes onto the court with the winner and they start to play. I sit down nearby, sensing myself not one of the guys. Quietly I move into the workout room where dozens of people are fixated on exercising with machines. The noisy Stairmaster, stationary bicycle, torso rotator, and treadmill are doing their jobs.

I position myself on the treadmill and begin a medium-paced jogging in place. *"Well, now that I'm warmed up, raring to play some more, that's it, squash is over for me tonight. Soon I have to go to work. I guess I want to run."*

My legs move rhythmically. I stare at a green light on the machine's panel. *"Well, that was interesting. Clearly, I'm not in their league. They were polite but wondering why I was there.*

Court Quest

The other women don't play at this time. They are still at work or fixing dinner for their kids. Or maybe they've learned they don't enjoy coming to Challenge Court and getting overpowered."

I continue my slow run on the treadmill. Sweat starts to drip off my forehead. I smile and wipe it away with the back of my hand, gazing at a white towel on a dark blue carpet next to the machine.

Competitive Spirit

I hold the phone to one ear as I riffle through the papers on my desk, searching for a pencil.

"No, Joy, I don't think I'm going to play in the City squash tournament. It's so much stress and I'm wanting another baby and at 42 I don't have much time."

"I see. Well, what about the in-house tournament, Tamara?"

"That I might play in. What I'd really like to do is go to Canada for the over 35 tournament you mentioned. That seems fair, to play other women closer to your age."

"Uh huh. Actually, I have the dates for the next Veterans tournament in British Columbia. Do you want them now?"

"OK."

"It's February 19-21 in North Vancouver. I'll let you know when I get a flyer with the details. In the meantime, shall we play this week?"

"Yes, let's. I have a nanny on Tuesday and Thursday, all day. How about Tuesday, the 12th, at 3:00 p.m.? I can't play at all in the morning. I have a hair appointment at 10:00, and I can't seem to get my son out and moving to the nanny before that. Then I have a horse riding lesson at 12:00 and have to pick up something for my husband at 1:30, but I could make it by 3:00."

Only halfway listening to my friend, I try to understand Tamara's life. It exemplifies my premise that women's lives are structured to lure them away, not towards, seriousness in something outside family life. Tamara could not become serious about squash unless something in her life shifted.

"Let's do 3:00. I'll get the court and call you if there's a problem. But let's not play hard, OK? I'm preparing for these tournaments, just gotta keep my timing up."

"Then maybe you don't want to play at all, before you compete."

"No, I've got to. If I don't, I lose my timing, my rhythm. I know from past experience."

"I kinda wish I were playing tournaments, Joy. I don't have time to train and I don't want to go out there and run out of breath. You know, what you need to do now is play with your heart, not drill or look at your weaknesses. Just prepare to go in there and play with your heart."

"I'll try."

"I really love that, playing with your heart. I played the Men's Round Robin the other night and was scared. My little heart was beating fast, but I played hard and was beating most of them. Their game is so different. But I like playing. You conquer your fear. You feel like a warrior. I like that feeling a lot. Most women squash players never get that feeling because most women don't play like we do. Some play on a team and they get that feeling a little, but it's not the same, it's not one-on-one. A warrior."

"Yep." I grin a little. "Just like old Boadicea."

"Who was she?"

"Queen of the Iceni, in Britain, around 62 A.D. She led a revolt against the Romans. A real fighter. Boadicea is also the name on the Women's Varsity shell for the University of Washington rowing team. I gotta go. See you tomorrow. Bye."

"OK. See ya, Joy. Bye."

I hang up and go to my athletic bag to sort out clothes for the wash. I look at my racquet strings and check them for signs of wear.

As I drive to the club I imagine Tamara looking at her legs, flexing them, touching them, sculpting on their muscles. I run over in my mind what I know about her.

She is muscular and has a cute laugh. She is a fast talker, emotionally expressive, and disclosing of what some would call personal information. She came relatively early to the New Feminism, and in her 20's and 30's was an assistant to a veterinarian. She and her older husband met when she was in her 30's. They became parents when she was "egg-mature."

Lightening and Lead

I am trying a Jazzercise class. The instructor is Jimmie, who is leading bench step patterns to loud music while shouting out commands via a microphone hooked around his neck. He is around 50 but looks ageless, and his classes are always packed.

"STEP STEP STEP STEP STEP STEP STEP STEP ONCE MORE STEP STEP STEP STEP KICK THIS ONE STEP STEP STEP STEP KICK STEP STEP STEP KNEE UP STEP STEP STEP KNEE UP STEP STEP STEP KEEP THOSE ARMS UP AND MOVING"

Stumbling over my big feet, I counsel myself: *"Oh damn.*

Why am I doing this to myself? I hate bench step aerobics. Always have, always will." I wipe away forehead sweat with the back of my hand. *"Look at these men and women, old and young. All working out hard. Look at that glimmer of glee in their eyes. They must be convinced this is good for them."*

Between gasping breaths I say to a sweating neighbor, "I don't know why I am trying this. Have never been able to finish an hour of bench aerobics. At least the music is cool." We grunt together and continue to flap our arms and legs.

"STEP STEP STEP STEP JUMPING JACKS STEP STEP STEP STEP   JUMPING JACKS   STEP STEP STEP STEP NOW FROZEN JACKS STEP STEP STEP STEP   FROZEN JACK FROZEN JACK"

Afterwards I telephone Rob at work. "Hi, it's me. Just checking in. I'm at the club."

"Oh hi. Say, you're up there, huh, how's it going?"

"OK. He really worked us."

"Then you'll be ready for us tonight, right?"

"Dreamer. Ready for a hot water bottle."

"Anyway, I'm kinda busy now. Let me call you later at home."

"OK. Ciao."

Later that day I play with Denise. She hits good shots, deep or front. I run after them and get them, move well, confidently stretch down and forward, jump up to reach high balls, twist, and hit to her deep backhand. I play swiftly, hard, and focused. After the match we shake hands and move off the court.

"Wow, Joy, what did you do? Take a pill? You were moving so much better than usual. I couldn't get it past you. Really, what's your secret?"

Court Quest

I make no comment but have a look of satisfaction on my face. Tossing the focus away from myself, I say, "Denise, you must have been a little...after your lesson."

"Yeah, after a session with Coach I always tend to think too much."

"Uh huh, instead of just playing, turning it on automatic."

"But I've never seen you move around the court so well."

Terry walks up. "Who won here?"

"I did. Three zip," I say as I wipe my racquet, neck, and face.

"I was thinking too much after my lesson. But, Terry, she was like lightening, getting all my balls."

"What's your secret?" he asks.

I smile. "Coffee and aerobics for lunch? Well, time to go! Thanks for the game, Denise. See you later."

"Bye!"

The next day I am on a court again but with totally different dynamics.

I walk on slowly, drill for warm-up, and hit with a random guy. Then he says, "Wanna play a few?"

"Sure, I'm just drilling, as you can see."

"I'm Alan. Remember me? The last time we played, you grilled me, seared me flat."

"Oh." I try not to let on that my memory about him is vague.

We play a game. Alan is aggressive and determined. I am almost punchy, not much stuffing there. I don't run. He hits drop shots. He gains the upper hand and wins.

I feel discouraged. As I towel off, I blank out and remember energetic lovemaking at night, languishing in the morning, reading, and studying. "So this is the price I must pay."

As I leave the club, I write a note to the tournament chairman, withdrawing from the in-house tournament, citing work schedule as a conflict. I do not give the real reason: fear of failure.

My life is erratic. I need to train daily. I need to schedule my other activities around my court life. I need to give up something. I am not doing what I need to reach the next skill level. I can't face my current reality in a tournament situation. My fragile identity as a superior female athlete is withering away.

I feel intense dread of not winning among my club peers. Everybody knows that I can beat the women who have entered this in-house tournament, but if I were to have an off day, I could lose.

"So there goes my opportunity to have my name in glory on the club plaque as the women's in-house tournament winner for this year. Oh well."

My discouragement is short-lived. The next day, feeling determined again, I get on a court, just to see how it is.

But I am stiff. Slow. Awkward. My reflexes are delayed. I am dull. I lose to a male D player who hasn't been playing the game very long.

"Is this what age brings? Spare me! May no one see me playing like this ever again! My pride! Old dumpy marshmallow! Out! Out!"

Hours later some other part of my brain goes into gear. *"Time for a counter move. What? Find something. Cross-training?"*

I make up a mantra based on the theme from the movie "Cool Runnings." It's about the Jamaican bobsled team that overcomes great odds to compete in the Winter Olympic Games in Calgary, Alberta.

I borrow their mantra:

Court Quest

"Keep your eyes on the prize!
Keep your eyes on the prize!
Keep your hand on the racquet!
Keep your hand on the racquet!"

Men's Draw

A man and his buddy are sitting on a bench outside the squash courts, fiddling with their eye guards and racquets. It isn't hard to overhear them.

"Who are you playing?"

"One of the women."

"Which one?"

"One of the older ones."

"Oh."

"I wonder why they're playing in our draw. Playing women in a squash tournament. Give me a break. What if I lose?"

"Oh, you won't lose. Just pound the ball at 'em."

"Why do they enter our draw? Don't they have their own?"

"Well, I guess not enough women signed up to fill out their own draw."

"Oh. Well, maybe we'll have lots of lets. I don't mind bumping into a good-lookin' woman on the court."

"Careful. You're sounding ripe for a sexual harassment charge."

"Oh, damn, better watch myself. I can imagine though, can't I?"

"You do that, and you might find yourself in the Consolation Round tomorrow. Get with it, man, these women can really play! They're not going to cut you any slack! You're going to have to win every point! And it won't do you any good looking at how their sport bra squashes their breasts all flat."

"Point well taken." He looks around.

"Time to get on the court for warm-up."

I watch them, fascinated. Stereotypes. Archetypes. I lapse into a kind of reverie.

I see Woman (Eve) on a court with Man (Adam). They are at the intermediate level, playing hard, doing lots of running. The referee (God) is perched above the court on a tall stool. He has a score sheet and a pencil in his hand. He is calling the score.

"8-7 left."

Man serves. Woman gets it back by playing scrappily. She wins the handout, the right to serve.

"7-8 serving right."

Woman serves well, but Man hits it very swiftly down the rail. She can't get there in time. Handout.

"8-7 serving right."

Man serves. This is a scrappy rally, too. The determination of Man and Woman blares out. Finally, Man wins the point.

"Point to Man. Game and match to Man."

They shake hands. Man looks very relieved. Woman looks jubilant. She put up a good fight and made him respect her. Man and Woman acknowledge the referee and walk off the court.

I am not sure if my vision means anything, but I think it is symbolic of some inner turmoil I face.

Woman, who is really Tamara, takes a drink of water from her bottle while toweling off. Denise has been watching this game, too.

"Great match! You really made him work for the win," exclaims Denise.

"Yeah, I'm just so pleased I was moving well and retrieving well. I'm tired though. He's a young buck, you know. And me, my legs hurt."

"Oh well, now you're in Consolations. You'll probably make it to the Finals there."

"If I can recover fast enough!"

Nearby, Tamara's opponent is engaged with his buddy. They are looking earnest.

"That gal, she had me worried there."

"Yeah, man. I was wondering when you were going to put her away. She's better than you thought she was, huh."

"Not only better, more determined than I expected."

"Then there's the other woman playing tonight. Heard she's pretty good, too. I may have to play her. I'd better watch her afternoon match."

"Good idea."

Later in the women's locker room, Tamara and Denise are slow to shower. I float quietly in the whirlpool tub and listen.

"You know, Denise, I wonder if I could get into shape enough so my legs wouldn't hurt. I think I could. But how long would it take? I do have a life. I want to get pregnant, and my husband and I, we're taking bridge lessons, and our son is at the age when he gets lots of attention."

"It's ironic. Once we're freed up from taking care of children, houses, and in some cases, husbands, we're so old we have to spend all our energy taking care of our carcasses!" Denise stretches and massages a knot out of her quadriceps.

"And by that time it's a little late to compete with the youngsters. Or is it? Who really knows?"

"That's why I think it's so neat, those 35-Plus tournaments they're having in Canada where you get to play your age group. I wish we had some of those around here."

"Yup, Tamara, if it's not one thing pulling you away from

the court, it's another. Competing with 20-year-olds is just not where it's at. Even the 30-Plus men face the age thing in squash. Did you see the match between that new old guy and the new young guy? The old man was the better player, but the young guy scrambled for everything, literally fell on the floor to make the gets, and eventually eked it out. The old man was crushed."

"Uh huh. I saw part of that one. Skill and savvy lost out to youth and quickness."

The two friends sit quietly awhile, and then Denise changes the subject.

"You know, I wonder what the real reason is that Joy isn't playing this in-house tournament. She was going to, and then pulled out."

"Well, she does work a couple of nights this week. Maybe she didn't want to deal with the scheduling problems. On the other hand, the last time we played, she wasn't playing well. She's very egotistical when it comes to squash. If she thinks she might lose, she won't play, or she won't play hard. She just looks cool on the court and gives in to her opponent's better playing. Sometimes she has an excuse."

"You may have something there. She did say she was tired of playing men and losing to them. She didn't sign up to play in the Men's draw if there wasn't a Women's draw."

"Oh, this is a problem. How can we get more women to play in tournaments?"

"Good question. A lot of women treat squash like a class they go to for exercise and fun."

"Especially the younger women with children. Not me, Denise, you know me—I love to compete and think I'm pretty good at it. If I'd started playing when I was eight, just think where I'd be by now—on the Women's World team!"

"But now with your son...."

"Yeah, you just can't. It's so hard to be consistent, to find the time. Remember the other day when we had a game set up and I had to cancel because my son suddenly got sick."

"I understand, really I do, even though I don't have children. Heck, now the men are beginning to relate to me as a squash player. Sometimes I wish they'd go back to seeing me as a woman who plays squash. I'd actually like to meet some single men in this town."

"Can't help you there, friend. Let's go get a cup of coffee. Oops, look at the time. I can't. Gotta go and pick up my son at his baby-sitter's."

After hearing them leave the locker room, I get out of the soothing tub, dress, and drive home without talking to anyone.

Mark Talbott Exhibition

On Wednesday I pop over to the club to watch Mark Talbott play an exhibition match with club pro Bruce Vinsonhaler. Mark is in his mid-twenties and a recent World Hardball Squash Champion. He is starting a squash academy in Newport, Rhode Island. Bruce is 40-something and a bit out of shape. The crowd watches the match enthusiastically.

Bruce plays well, gets some points, and peppers the event with humor, good sportsmanship, and some fine playing. Mark runs well and has a startling array of shots. Between games Mark comments on Bruce's play and their court interaction. Mark says that we are lucky to have Bruce as our coach, that he has a clean and skillful style. To close off the evening Mark demonstrates how to drill by yourself.

The next day I see Coach as he is about to give a lesson to Trish Quinn whom I have just played.

"Bruce, I saw your game with Mark. How are you feeling?"

"Yeah it was, whatever."

"Trish and I just finished a reverse copy of your match with Mark. She was Mark, the one who retrieved everything."

Laughing, we get some mileage out of the fact that Mark made Bruce run and that the age difference was operating. Age is something we have to joke about. We part with smiles exchanged.

Training Pay-off

Thanks to Cindy, I am in a little better shape. Cindy is a tough yet friendly aerobics and strength instructor who volunteers as a firefighter in a small town just outside of Seattle. Even though I am the only one in the afternoon class who plays squash, Cindy includes training that would benefit a squash player's muscles and flexibility. Thanks to Cindy's rigorous approach and my consistent attendance, my overall fitness is up. I have noticed a change in the way my flesh hangs on my thighs—less rubbery, less pockety, less dimpled, less like cottage cheese.

Women's Squash Program

Hilary Thomas has decided not to coach us anymore. In exchange for coaching she gets a free membership and access to the club's amenities. She is an Open level player, competed in college, and is a young professional. We have looked forward to our hours of coaching and playing with Hilary. When she announced she was no longer going to make the long drive from her home to the club, we were not pleased. Nevertheless, we have decided to do our Saturday morning Round Robin without Hilary. It is our first attempt to organize ourselves.

This day we are able to get our spirits up and play each other. We have a few laughs and some healthy sweat. As a lark I play a C level woman with my right hand. She wins, but I get some points.

Once I surprise onlookers by getting to a distant ball, and Tamara says, "That just proves it. If Joy can get to it, she can do something with it." I grunt and stay focused. As the morning goes on, I hit some brilliant shots, especially when I have to bend low, stretch out, and extend forward on my forehand.

We miss the coaching Hilary usually gives us—the tips, the cautions, the observations, the drills, and the sense of belonging to a group of serious players. We wonder if it would do any good to appeal to the club's director.

"What do you think about this Women's Squash Program, Denise?"

"I'm not sure what you mean, Joy."

"Well, I sense it is dissolving. It is limping along. I'm a serious player, and now I'm feeling anxious about doing squash seriously."

"Oh, I see what you mean. It is not the same since Hilary stopped coaching us."

"Sometimes it's easy to see how much we could improve, and then the feeling of uneasiness intensifies."

"Yes, I think I know what you're getting at."

"Something similar has happened to other women's

sport programs I've been in, Denise. Feels like a repeat. Here today, gone tomorrow. What is the future of women's club squash in the 1990's?"

"I don't know. It depends."

On a personal front I have clarity. I need to prepare for the tournament this weekend in Canada and I am serious about trying to play well. Even if the women's program falters, I must not. I must hit every day until I leave. Hilary's exit disturbs me, but I don't think it is a fatal blow. Our head coach is very competent and is there for me when I am ready to take lessons. I am not yet ready.

I have let the regulars know I am competing in Canada and that by playing with me, they are helping me train. A few of them show a slight interest in what I am doing.

The next day I play twice to see how it will be to play twice in a day, since that is most likely what I will have to do this coming Saturday in Canada. I pretend I am playing a real match and take only 90 seconds between games. To my surprise I play very well—perhaps the best I have ever played softball squash. When I blister a forehand cross-court, observer Terry shakes his head a few times in awe and disbelief. Today squash does not seem arduous to me.

As I leave for home, I run into Terry.

"Terry, I heard you were going to the tournament in Canada this weekend."

"No, huh, I thought about it, then I got injured, so I'm not, but I'd like to, really would. Are you going?"

"Yes."

"What are you going to play?"

"Women's 45-49 B."

"You are going to kick butt!"

I have been drinking wheat grass juice prepared in my blender. Am I experiencing an extra zing from this juice? Is "menopausal zest" kicking in?

Skill and Cunning Vets Tournament
Evergreen Squash Club
Vancouver, British Columbia, Canada

I win. Three hard matches. The second match is the hardest. I am down six match points in the fifth game and come back to win the game and the match!

At my sentimental request, my opponent in this hardest match, Diane Harskamp, age 40, graciously signs the score sheet, as does the referee, for me to keep as a souvenir.

Basically, Diane wins the first game by cutting off my service returns for winners. I try various serves to see what she handles well. Somehow, in the second game I hit it where Diane isn't and get my winners. Also, my hard serves give her trouble. (Instead of waiting for the ball to bounce, Diane should step into it and volley it.)

The third game Diane wins in a tiebreaker. The fourth game I win in a tiebreaker.

The courts are very cold. For this match I am wearing my old beige figure skating tights. They help me stay warm and flexible. Most importantly, they take away the fear of scraping my legs on the court if I scramble for a ball. In this match I do scramble—a lot—to the gasps of the onlookers. My reward is some points and handouts. I spend about as much time in contact with the court floor as one expects of an inexperienced twenty-something male player.

For the fifth game I have the serve and get the first two points. Then I serve a lob that Diane demolishes. Diane gets

Skill and Cunning Vets Tournament

the handout to serve and pulls out a string of winners, mostly by hitting short. I do not get to the ball in time. She also hits deep and makes me run front to back, or midcourt to back. Now I am down 2-8 in the last game, at match point. Somehow I get the handout and serve for a string of points, making it 8-8. Diane calls two points to win. I take a deep breath and serve hard, fast, deep, and low. Diane can't handle it. Point to me. I do the same serve again from the other side. Point to me. I win!

I have planned well and trained hard. My mental toughness is there and my will to win is tops. I am in no mood to lose to lesser skilled players or even equally skilled players. Basically, I edge out these women through focus and when I have to, just gutting it out. If I keep up this pace, let the instinctive anticipation roll, run well, hit the ball where they aren't, and hit hard enough, the matches will swing my way.

No one is around to distract me. Before matches I don't chatter and I don't eat, except for a Power Bar. I limber up, stretch out, and pulse up. I do all the recommended things, such as checking my equipment and tying my shoelaces in double knots.

Many of these women are busy helping with the tournament between their matches. For them it is a social as well as an athletic event. Some husbands are here, watching their wives' matches, giving advice. Diane's husband was in the stands, shouting out advice like a Dad at his kid's soccer match. Does a husband's presence distract a woman?

I am used to going it alone and by now I prefer it that way. There is some moral support, however. As I left Seattle, Rob told me to drive safely and then said pseudo gruffly, "See that you WIN." His voice—these words—this command—came back to me as I was setting to serve and needed the point desperately. But he isn't here in reality. When I want him to be there for me, I call up his virtual reality in my mind and receive what he gives me.

As I head out of Vancouver, I enjoy the comfort of my prize for first place in my age group—a warm-up suit of nice colors, cozy, large enough, and well made. My brain is slow, my left arm is sore, and I walk funny. I am relieved that I have finally won a squash tournament, albeit in my age group. It has been a long time since I have won something. I am moving up. No longer am I being knocked out in the first round of play. No longer am I a Finalist or Consolations winner. Finally, I am a winner, at age 49 and 11 months.

When I see Rob again, I tell him about the weekend and show him the signed score sheet. He grins and gives me a jubilant hug. "Way to go!"

Some time during the drive back from Vancouver, a song strikes my brain:

"Menopausa Momma"

Oh, I'm a menopausa momma,
A menopausa momma,
A menopausa momma,
You better watch out for me.

Oh I'm a menopausa momma,
A menopausa momma,
A menopausa momma,
You better watch out for me.

Skill and Cunning Vets Tournament

Oh, you better watch out for me,
You better watch out for me,
Cuz I'm a menopausa momma,
A menopausa momma,
A menopausa momma,
Just waiting to be free.

Back in Seattle I sing part of this song to my squash buddies and they grin. They congratulate me on my win. My nature being what it is, I take the pleasure of telling my squash coach, the swim coach, the fitness trainers, and all my squash buddies about this triumph.

My mind flushes with gratitude for legs that let me run, lungs that work, and a will that wants. Now I get to plan out the next phase of my long effort.

Not one to get uppity and complacent, I note what I need to learn and how I can improve. For instance, when I am in the front court waiting for my opponent to hit the ball, I must look at *her*, not the front wall. If I hit a loose ball into a corner and it caroms towards the center, often I get stuck in front of my opponent who calls for a let and gets awarded a stroke. Learning to move in a curvy banana pattern away from the ball would be smart.

Puget Sound Tournament
YMCA and Tacoma Lawn and Tennis Club
Tacoma, Washington, USA

Some weeks later I decide to play in a tournament in the U.S. that does not have age groups. I am primed to risk playing some younger women.

The tournament takes place a half hour drive from Seattle. It's a popular tournament and is packed with men and women of all ages from the Pacific Northwest.

Walking around the courts, I see sweat on player's faces, wet T-shirts clinging to backs, and racquets up in nervous anticipation of a coming serve. Referees are focused and business-like, calling scores, recording scores, deciding lets, strokes, and handouts. Players are asking for lets by voice and by gaze. Referees are saying, "Let," "No let," or "Yes, stroke."

A bright black ball flies slowly through the air and glances against a smudged and spattered white wall. It bounces once and then is scooped up by a short player. The ball takes on personality. Right then it enjoys being run after and scooped up.

On this Saturday after their matches, players mingle in the club's lounge. The setting is luscious and luxurious. The grand old building is made of reddish brick, the grounds are lined with tall, old trees, and the walls shine of burnished hardwood. On the walls and in display cases are memorabilia highlighting the wealthy men who started this club almost a hundred years ago with their railroad, timber, and gold money.

People are milling around a buffet table, eating and

drinking. On the wall a television set broadcasts inaudibly a pro basketball game. The crowd is mostly men. I decide to sit next to a woman I know. While eating, I find myself curious and prompting conversation.

"Well, how old are you, Mari?"

"Twenty-nine."

"That's a hard age. But if you're not settled yet, and you're still sputtering around, maybe you don't notice it."

"Well, I guess I do. But I just figure when it happens for me, it happens. I just came out of a four-year relationship, and I'm doing what's best for me."

"When I was 29, I was deeply in love, had just had my son, and was starting to play squash."

"Yeah, now I wish I had started playing when I was younger."

"Me too."

"Anyway, someday I would like to do the family thing, have children."

"Well, I wonder who the single men are around here."

"I don't know. They don't tell."

"I think they have a hard time seeing women who are serious about their sport as female. You know what I mean?"

"Yeah, it's like they don't look at you. They think you're one of the guys."

"Uh huh, I wonder if they're a little intimidated and don't know how to act toward a woman they sense doesn't want to be, you know, treated in the traditional way. All this sexism stuff nowadays has perplexed a bunch of them, I think."

"Yeah, I bet you're right! But I want them to see me as a woman, too. If we're walking through the door, I want them to open the door for me."

"And flirting is fun."

"Yeah, flirting. But Joy, who does that anymore— except the woman who's around the court to catch a man. You can kinda tell, you know, which ones are."

"Do you think the men are sophisticated enough to know the difference? I've noticed they kind of give up and treat all women squash players the same."

"Oh, I think some of them know— like Wade. He's such a cynic. Anything that comes out of him, I know is *something*."

"What did he say that makes you say this, Mari?"

"The other day I was playing and Wade was watching. After our match, he said to this other guy, who told me later, 'You know, Mari's here not just to look good; she's here to play well.'"

"He actually said that?"

"Yes."

"Unbelievable. It's as though he finds it astonishing that a woman is bent on doing her sport well."

I nod as Mari moves on to talk with someone else.

I sit alone. I wonder where my opponent is. It's getting late. My envisioning presses into my near future. Yes, I will have to play my nemesis. But Mariza is almost late, now she is late, now the tournament director is asking around about her. Someone thinks she is stuck in a traffic jam due to a big car accident. *Not only is she stuck, she is part of the accident and has been injured seriously. She will be unable to play in this tournament or any tournament for many months. Thus by default my nemesis is no longer an obstacle on my path!*

Lo, it is not to be. Mariza arrives. We play. I win the first game and in the second game I am up 8-3. I lose game point, lose that game, and the next two games. I lose the

Puget Sound Tournament

match. My nemesis wins 3-1.

I am disgusted with myself. I had a chance against this woman and botched it. What is my problem? I am not sure. I return home, don't talk to Rob, and hide in my bed as long as I can.

Sunday is the day of final matches for other players and the third round of matches in our Women's B Round Robin. On center court I am playing Sue Lehr who played very well Saturday. She beat Mariza in five games. Then Mariza played Cindy Merritt and won in five games. Since both Mariza and Cindy beat me, it is logical that Sue would beat me.

I plan a strategy and it works. I play a hard serve match with fast running to the front, controlling the front court, and keeping Sue back. I lob well to her deep backhand and make no unforced errors. Instead of taking my serve to her backhand on the volley, she lets it drop and too often gets caught with a low bounce. I am clicking and she is a little off.

Primed from playing the day before, I notch it up a little. Playing on center court where a crowd is waiting for something to happen catalyzes my desire to show myself as part of this squash scene. I want to do what my club mates would delight in, what Denise asked for when I asked her if she would sub for me, since I wasn't quite prepared to play two tournaments in two weekends. In declining my request, Denise ordered, "Do me a favor, beat Sue Lehr." I beat her 3-0.

By this match I spark higher into the local squash scene. Now I am part of the competition, someone to be reckoned with, not just an old player pitifully trying to make a mark, not just a deluded woman who is spending her time, effort, and money for nothing. Respect of players matters and I am glad to get nice comments from several advanced players.

I watch another match. Sue Clinch, a National Age Group 35-Plus Champion, is playing hard. Mostly she plays men. She is very fit, very trim, and is wearing white parachute-silk shorts that cling to her moist skin.

Clinch and her opponent play to a tiebreaker in the fifth game of the Men's B Championship. She tins one too many and loses by one point. Her play against Scott from Spokane, Washington, is glorious, valiant and beautiful. She has remarkable fitness, poise, focus, and skill.

Later in the locker room Sue asks about my match, and then upon being prompted, says her match was a good match. "A good work out, which is what I wanted." Such is her self-effacing comment after playing four matches the day before and winning the Women's A Final a few hours before playing her Men's B Final! I am amazed at how other-directed she is in small talk. How does such a trait fit with her drive to excel on the court?

At home, I visualize Sue's postures as she reaches for shots. Can I ever copy them? She is the best player in the Seattle area, except for the young Open player, Shabana Khan.

Ambivalence

My high from the Tacoma tournament doesn't last long. My seesawing about squash continues. On the ambition side, I hit with a guy on Friday night and Saturday morning. It is much more challenging to hit with men than women because men hit harder and faster and I need to quicken my reflexive reactions.

On the other hand, I am not sure I want to keep up this intensity and frequency of competing. Recently when I played Tamara and did fine, I garnered some praise. "Joy, you played SMART." That's nice, but is it worth the effort?

It is logical to enter the upcoming City Championships. I have been considering not entering in order to save money and to give myself an excuse for going away during spring break.

How strongly am I feeling an obligation to compete in a local tournament, especially if I am playing well? I am sensing some expectation from club members to play. This is the first time I have felt such an expectation. In a way the pressure makes me want to walk away. My waffling about entering the upcoming tournament is another instance of my inconsistency. The lure back into slothfulness is magnetic. But my ambitious part tells me I have to venture out or shrink. In order to get interesting matches I have to play tournaments.

At the next Women's Round Robin I hit with Hilary for a few minutes. She has decided to coach us when she can, that is, when she doesn't have pressing work and isn't overly tired from her workload. I love hitting with her again. We drill backhand volley returns and some movement strategy. I decide I need private lessons.

Just as Hilary returns, my favorite conditioning class departs. Cindy's daytime class is canceled due to relatively low numbers. So it becomes more difficult for me to attend a class that suits my timetable and my needs for workout, stretching, and strength. Without this particular class, I am more apt to slack off.

Suddenly eager for change, I toy with moving out of Level B into Level A for my age group. The Canadian women in B's have mentioned this to me. They want a chance to win the B's. I want to be in a higher level of play. Even though the softball version of squash racquets is still new to me, I believe I have improved and can improve more. Some lessons teaching me to hit deeper would help.

Most older American squash players learned to play on narrow courts with a hard rubber ball. The international game is played on wider courts with a softer ball that stays up in the air longer after being hit. Different techniques in hitting, positioning, and moving are required.

The B's are nobody worth emulating. Sometimes the B's produce a good match, but generally B level play, men or women, is lower quality than the A level. Of course, ever getting to the Open level at my age is unrealistic. Even if I lose in the A's, which I will, moving up is a good idea.

If I do enter the upcoming city tournament—B's or A's—I will have to do it without Rob around. He is leaving shortly for his spring vacation. I have never gotten used to separations from him. I want to go places with him, but that is impossible. I am continuously putting psychic energy into coping with our arrangement; energy once used up is gone and cannot be used for utilitarian matters such as training.

Decision

"Hello?"

"Hello, Joy? This is Yusef. About the City Championships. We don't have enough to make an Age Group Women's draw. We're trying to put you in the B's. Would you like to play in the B's?"

"Not really. That's too bad. I made up my mind that I

Decision

don't want to play if the 35-Plus draw doesn't go. Sorry about that!"

"That's OK. Maybe next time. We'll return your check."

"Thanks, bye."

I hang up and breathe a sigh of relief. *"Now I can get out of town for my spring vacation. Take a break from squash. With Rob gone for two weeks, staying around here will be dismal. Time to do something different, help keep my spirits up."*

Later that day Tamara and I are playing. "I need a new racquet, Joy. You see the strings on this? They're ready to go. My husband wants me to get it re-strung, but I want a racquet like yours, with a bigger sweet spot."

"Yeah, this one has more spring, too. It's easier to hit long shots."

"Joy, I still don't know how much squash I want to play and how hard. I love to win. I want to train and get better. But we're doing the baby thing again. We're going in for more tests next week. I want to get aggressive about it. The doctors are talking about artificial insemination of my husband's sperm. He's had a test; his count is OK, about average. The doctor thinks it might help to make sure those little thingies get where they're supposed to get."

"Well, I guess you have to decide what is most important to you at this time."

"Right, and I do love squash, and especially since you've come to the club, I have more competition. You're my main competition now."

"Yes. Gotta have someone your level to play with. Well, you ready? I'm starting to get cooled off."

"OK. Let's play!"

During a Men's Round Robin I am sitting around. As directed by Coach, I am there to play with men of various levels.

Coach tells me to play Steve Pulliam. We walk onto a court.

"Hey, Joy. How are you playing today?"

"I'm makin' them sweat. I'll make you earn your points."

We play a game. We sweat, run, hit, crash into each other, groan, and laugh. Afterwards Steve says, "Say, I've got a court for Saturday after the Women's Round Robin, but no one lined up yet. Do you want to?"

"Hum. I guess I could do that. I'll be tired, but I'll plow through it, make you run."

"OK, see you then."

So Saturday between games Steve and I are resting on a bench. Our T-shirts are hot and sweaty and we smell bad.

"Steve, I'm thinking of going to Canada in two weeks for a Masters tournament. Do you play tournaments in Canada?"

"Nah, I'm not much of a tournament player. I just play around here. I'm not in that good a shape."

"But you play a lot here at the club," I counter.

"Yes, I can't do without squash. But to really get into tournament shape, I'd have to train better—run—you know, the works. I'm pretty busy at work, too."

I nod. We look at each other with respect and no obvious man-woman interest. Our mutual passion for squash is obvious. Suddenly I am aware that my dream-wish has popped to the surface again. I yearn for a man to play squash with and go to tournaments with. This is not the man, though.

After spending a few days at a Quaker retreat, I am curious about the City tournament I did not enter, so I call Denise.

"Hi, Denise, this is Joy. I'm back in town. How'd you do in the tournament?"

"I won the Consolations! Yeah, I played Mariza on Friday and lost to her in 4, then played Kristie and Jan on Saturday and won easily."

"Congratulations!"

"Guess who won it? Kate, the woman you beat in the Seattle Open last year, the one who ran into your racquet. She was really motivated. Shelley, she played, even though she was running the tournament. She didn't play that well, said she was tired, so Kate got the edge."

"Groan—if I'd stayed and played the B's, I probably could have won it!"

"Or at least been a Finalist."

"Oh well, that was my decision. OK, so let's talk about playing this week."

Later in a moment of introspection, I talk back to myself like an older brother chiding a little sister: *"Where is my motivation? My drive? My goal to play all tournaments for the experience? To lead up to a good ranking for a favorable draw at Nationals? To learn more about playing tournaments in order to be better prepared for Nationals?"*

I sigh, unsure of what part of me is talking and where the words and tone are coming from.

Gloom

It is one of those 4:30 wake-up mornings when you don't know what you want.

Court Quest

But Tamara knows. She has found out she is pregnant. She is very happy. She showed me the two little blue dots on the pregnancy tester and called herself "an egg on legs."

Tamara doesn't play very fiercely and so our match is easy and pleasant. For me her condition means the woman who is most challenging at this club is out of commission. I am genuinely happy for her and find it interesting how disclosing she is about personal matters. This news gets me reflecting again on my years of wanting a second child, but I feel no traumatic overlay, that is, I have successfully suppressed my traumatized part.

My discernible distress comes forth during my mini-lesson with Coach when he discusses my swing, especially my back swing. Last week an opponent who was standing behind me felt the sting of my racquet on her lips during my follow-through.

Coach insists, "Standing in back of an opponent is supposed to be safe. A swing should extend forward and up, not around and back. This kind of swing happens when you are in the heat of battle. Listen carefully, Joy, the spring wind-up comes *before* the hit, then the player unwinds and follows through *forward*." His description makes sense and means I have to change my stroke. "I don't know if I can! But I have to!"

The follow-through I had in hardball squash doesn't cut it in softball squash. No doubt my hardball swing was inefficient and dangerous, too. My tendency to turn my wrist over and bend my elbow so the racquet head ends up near my own head is not good.

Some women don't like to play with me for fear of getting hit. Especially if they forget I am left-handed, they aren't aware of where they are in relation to my swing. The

Gloom

fact that I hit harder and faster than any woman in the club has also made less experienced women shy away from playing me. They feel intimidated, whereas a man of the same skill level and experience doesn't. Even though I have been clearing better and causing fewer lets, my reputation stays. New habits based on better technique are needed.

How to develop a better style at my age? While I don't want to play with players I can beat all the time, I also don't want to play with those I always get beat by. Too often I end up with a sensation of battle rather than fun. I need more racquet and positioning skills and would like to experience my performance as more graceful, seemingly effortless. Like a dancer.

When playing certain players, I could elect not to hard serve, and instead, dip around playfully with lob serves and drop shots, something I like doing. But how would doing this help me improve my game? Actually, developing new serves is a good idea. Perfecting drops and nicks would be smart. Easier said than done.

Coach talks with me about playing more men and more regularly. At first I resist this approach. I haven't made much attempt to know the men here. I can't go to Men's Round Robin because I work that night, and none of those guys are likely to call me for a match.

Discouragement displays itself again. As to my goal of playing in the United States Nationals— it is still there, but a plan for taking the steps to get there eludes me. I don't want to go out of town for a big tournament like Nationals unless my game is better, especially my return of good serves. Of course, controlling my swing is part of the competency I need. I doubt I can afford private lessons—which is what I wish for.

49

My lack of resolve, discipline, and clarity as to how to proceed shows up in traditional ways, for me. A huge vat of chocolate chip cookie dough in my freezer is almost gone. I will be astonished when it is empty. I kid myself that if I eat it frozen and raw, I will get sick of it sooner than if I bake it into cookies.

Bouncing Back

Now I am training with Cindy again, since her fitness class has been re-instated one day a week. Although I feel pleased with this development, what good is it if I am fit and trim but can't get enough squash, can't play more safely, and can't take lessons so I can get better?

Recently Cindy's class has been very tough. We do squat back push-ups and push-downs as well as push-ups on bent knees. The aerobic segment is grueling, too. The day after a class I have severe soreness of triceps, calf muscles, and muscles back of my knees. A day later, I feel strong and usable again. I am glad I have refused to give up.

I am playing men almost exclusively. I play Alan a good match and he wins. We play smoothly and I play with more flair and less control than usual. The consequence is reduced accuracy, mostly on crosscourt drives. No matter, it's good to try different approaches.

I don't really care what the men think of me when I play them. I like it, though, when I overhear someone making a comment about my squash. When I hear a guy refer to "her blistering forehand from mid-court," I take note.

In the past when Tamara and I played and the guys walked past the glass-walled courts, they glanced in and said, "Clash of the Titans!" Now that Tamara is pregnant and pampering her aggressiveness on the court, we no longer hear such a comment.

To save money and spend time on getting better, I pass up small tournaments around town. For a change of pace I join the University of Washington Sailing Club and sail across Puget Sound to Blake Island. "Snooze N' Booze" is an overnight event put on by the local sailing club that has nothing to do with squash! For a few hours I am seen not as a middle-aged woman trying to prop up her squash game, but rather, a middle-age woman trying to learn to sail. Sigh.

Inspiration

The Speaker is the Reverend Bill Gray. The place is the First Baptist Church on the Brown University campus in Providence, Rhode Island. Inside the church my son is seated in full graduation regalia with his classmates. Family and friends are seated on the grass outside, listening via loudspeakers. Reverend Gray's voice is deep and solid:

"Now your answers will be questioned. You're on your own. The challenge is to dance to all the music of life. Take in the three virtues—faith, hope, and love. Faith in the future prevents shortsightedness. Hope comes from the spirit, the soul, and helps us dance. Love is the universal hunger to fill the God-shaped vessel within. Without love we are not free to reach beyond our own narrow self-interests. Celebrate and dance today of life that is given to you. And know these three things—faith, hope, and love abide, but the greatest of these is love." *(I Corinthians 13:13)*

During this address my love of *squash* surfaces and I

take inspiration from it, the speaker, and the occasion.

Back home at a Men's Round Robin, Tamara, Rock, and I are chatting. Rock looks at me. "I understand your son just graduated from Brown University."

"Yes. Did you go to Brown?"

"No, I went to Washington State. But anybody who can get into and graduate from Brown earns my complete admiration."

"And look, she's the Mom, looks just like a babe herself!" says Tamara, grinning.

Could it be that fitness training and squash playing slow down the aging thing?

Some players are talking about what it is like to play various people. Someone asks Tamara about my game. "Oh, she's beatable. All you have to do is drug her." Someone else says, "Yeah, when she warms up, she's a killer." I lap up anything I hear about my game. I am hungry to know what I am like.

Playing Men

One way to find out more about myself is to play men and contrast my playing style to theirs. One day Dennis and I are playing—it's very close. We hit swift strokes on a hot court. The score is 8-8 and then 9-8 for Dennis. Coach watches, smiles, and talks to us through the glass back wall.

"Whoa, Abe, if it weren't for those three-walls, you'd be dead meat."

"He had three of 'em this game," says Coach, looking at me.

"Yeah. Uh, what's the defense against a three-wall?"

Coach doesn't say anything.

"Watch," pipes up Dennis.

"You have to get up there!" says Coach finally.

"People can DO that?" I groan, lamenting my natural slowness and inability to spurt off the block.

On the same evening Rock and a new player are talking about playing me. "Um, Rock, about her, how's her game?"

"She doesn't move very well, but she hits it harder than anyone I know."

"You talking about me?" I ask.

"Yeah, I told him you hit it harder than anyone I know."

I detect a slight mockery in his voice. He walks onto a court and I think to myself, *Obviously you mean any WOMAN you know.*"

Later Coach pairs me with the new guy. "Tim, we'll throw you to the sharks, even though you're a new guy. Joy, you play Tim here." Coach grins.

We play and it is really no contest, not fair to the new guy.

At the next Men's Round Robin Tim and I play again. Before starting our game, we shake hands and Tim says, "I'm better than I was last week when we played."

"Oh?"

"Uh, I played twice and had a lesson."

Our match is a showcase of inexperience versus experience. I meet his big, wide back swing by ducking and staying out of his way. Coming up with a variety of serves and smart shots, I play easily, quickly, efficiently, steadily, and seriously. When we finish at 9-0 mine, we shake hands, exit the court, and walk over to Coach. Coach looks at me and says, "Pulled out all the stops, eh?" For all of my emotional intelligence, I can't quite put my finger on the tone behind his comment.

Adjustments

Tamara's pregnancy ends with a miscarriage. She is sad and disappointed, but intends to try again after a healing period.

While Tamara and her husband have to adjust to their loss, I have to adjust to Rob's absence from Seattle for most of the summer. It is something I have to accept. I don't discuss him with my squash buddies. They know about him, but have never met him. He is a mystery man. My feelings about his absence are, as usual, hidden deeply away.

A Quickie Tournament

Wade is holding court around the club's bulletin board, explaining the grid that shows handicap points for all the entrants. Handicap points are determined by a combination of playing level, age, and gender.

"Now, Joy, you play Michael here, and you get some points. You're level B, add two points for gender, then add age points. How old are you?"

"Fifty."

Wade looks sideways at me. "Bull—."

"You could have fooled me!" says a nearby staff member.

"Well, so you add two points for age, but he's 40, so he gets one point, so subtract one. His handicap is seven points. American scoring, to 15."

"OK, here we go!"

"Sock it to him, gal!" someone shouts.

The atmosphere is relaxed. Beer and pop are in a cooler and in some hands. All but three players are men. We see some good play between men and women with women pulling out some points and games. Some men make silly unforced errors and feel embarrassed. Tonight the razzing is particularly intense.

Between matches Denise, Tamara, and I shoot the breeze.

"It's hot. I took my son swimming this morning at Lake Washington. It was crowded," says Tamara.

"You should take him to my son's beach for swimming. He's a lifeguard. He'd be glad to meet him, pay attention to him," I say.

"Which beach is that?"

"Madison Park."

"Would I recognize him?"

"I doubt it. He doesn't look anything like me. He's dark-complected. Tall."

"Is your husband dark?"

"Uh huh. My son is too, and tall, good smile, really broad shoulders, wears a 44-46 jacket."

"And a small waist," adds Denise, who used to swim competitively in college.

I glance at her quickly. "A 32 inch waist!"

"Is he single?"

I look surprised. "Yes."

Suddenly Denise looks sheepish. "How old is your son?"

"Twenty-one."

"Denise!" says Tamara affectionately.

Denise flushes a little and we chide her a bit more. It would be convenient for her to fall for some guy on the squash court. Where are the good ones?

We get ready to leave. "Joy, are you going to the Women's Round Robin tomorrow?"

"Uh huh. Are you?" says Denise.

"No, I don't think so. I have to go to a Jewish ceremony

for a new baby boy."

"Oh, do you want to? You could come for a little while to play, and be late for your—"

"Uh, I don't think so. The father of this baby is a good friend of mine."

"The father? How about the mother?"

"Oh, her a little. He's an ex-boyfriend of mine and we're good friends. I keep my old boyfriends."

"Oh? How do you do it?"

"I never see them AND I never ask them for money!! Bye now!"

Summer Wonderings

It is full summer now. Tamara, Denise, Hilary, and I are loafing around the courts. We watch a group of men walking down the hall near the courts.

"Tamara is always introducing me to single men," says Denise.

"Why not?" I ask.

"Sometimes it feels a little obvious."

"Oh well," says Tamara, "nothing ventured, nothing gained. You do talk about being single all the time."

"I know, it's just that I—."

"I know how you feel," says Hilary. "Every time I break up with my boyfriend, I think to myself, I don't want to go through it all again, meeting someone, that is."

"It's odd that you haven't met someone around the club you're attracted to," I venture. "They say that playing sports together is a good way to stay together."

"Oh, forget it. It's getting too hot to play squash," says Denise. "This place needs air-conditioning. What else is there to do on weekends around here?"

"Hiking," says Hilary. "I have done a little hiking this year, but not as much as I want."

"How do you decide where to go?" asks Denise.

"I get those books—hiking books. Have done some alpine lakes. It's pretty nice to have a lake at the top of your hike, so if you're sweaty, you can cool off, refresh yourself."

"Do you go by yourself?" asks Tamara.

"Some. There's one person I go with sometimes, but I have gone by myself. I'd sooner go by myself than stay home on a Sunday, after working hard all week."

"Have you run into any danger?" I inquire.

"Not really. Once I went up in June, there was still snow on the trail, in parts, and I kinda lost the trail. I thought, 'Darn, I'm here by myself and snow is hiding the trail.'"

"Not real wise," says Tamara.

"Well, if you ever want to go with someone, give me a call," says Denise.

"OK, that could be fun. Uh—do you run trails? I run them and bike them."

"Are you kidding?" responds Denise.

We laugh heartily and I interject, "Hilary, if you want to SAUNTER up a trail, you can call me."

We laugh again.

"Well," says Tamara, "Come on, Joy, let's play. I'm not going to get any warmer than I already am."

Tamara continues. "Hey, you guys, let's go to Nationals. When is it?"

"Second week of October, October 8th to 11th," says Hilary.

"In San Francisco? I love it down there."

"Not me. I'm not going. Haven't been playing," says Hilary.

I look outwards and say, "Nationals. That was one of my

long-term goals when I joined this club."

Hilary and Tamara look at me knowingly.

Tamara changes the subject. "I'm thinking of going back to school. I want to do something different, something with my hands. Joy, you sail. Are engines on sailboats diesel?"

"I only know about outboard engines on sailboats and they are gasoline. Why?"

"I want to become a diesel marine mechanic."

It is a summer of no summer in the Pacific Northwest. Solid rain and gray skies disturb the city for two months. By September we are still pale and washed out.

Tamara miscarries again. She begins to express herself in terms of, "My son, he may be my only child," rather than, "When I have a second child."

Denise defends her dissertation well and is happy about that. Her next hurdle is to "publish or perish."

Hilary continues to work long hours in a small town. At thirty-something, she, like Denise, is feeling the age thing.

I go to my family's lake cabin in Idaho. It is a peaceful place and I return refreshed.

None of us women go to Nationals in San Francisco. A few men from our club fly down. They play well but win nothing. A handful of men and women from the Seattle Club go. My nemesis Mariza goes. She plays well but doesn't win her age group.

School starts and Denise, Rob, and I start teaching. For me teaching is not enough. I want something more and different. I don't know what I am capable of, what I want. I notice that customer service women still call me "Hon." I wonder whether I come on as immature and needy.

"What about Masters Nationals next spring?" I muse.

Feeling Sorry for Myself

Sniffing onto Rob's shoulder, I whine, "I'm only a Wannabee."

"Are you only a Wannabee?" he asks. "Why don't you think the word 'Winner'? Why do you continue to get distracted? Why this zigzag course?"

I don't answer because I can't.

Two aspects of my life mean I have to bolster myself continuously against strong outside forces. First, an unjust employment situation still pummels me. After decades of teaching almost full-time at community colleges and university, I still have a low salary, no retirement-fund eligibility, and a career entrenchment that leads nowhere. Also, an unusual love life still catches me. After a quarter of a century with Rob, our relationship and his relationship with our son are still incomplete. I want to get married to him and live happily ever after, something not in the cards for him. At times these two realities of job and love cause my spirit to sag. A sagging spirit means avoiding squash. Simply wishing I could change things isn't effective.

Focusing on what I can influence is gratifying. I have plenty of time to choreograph in my mind what kind of sport life I would like. My fantasy is to have a personal coach, a friend, a manager— to do the planning and the pushing. I am willing to go through the physical and mental strain of full-scale training towards excellence. If only there were someone to help me. But really, does it matter that a 50-year-old woman plays squash at the high B or the low A level? Does it matter that she has a goal and tries to reach it? Will anyone notice if she becomes a hotshot squash player? Does anyone really care?

I am halfway into my fiftieth year. I think I am among

the top five players in my age group in the USA. In Canada I am not sure. People say that when they see me playing well, they forget my age.

A New Season

When I get back from vacation, knowing I am rusty, I go to the Challenge Court. I play with Terry on a different court. I don't move well until our last game. I don't worry about playing poorly. I accept a natural return to the game. Fewer guys than usual show up, and I am the only woman. Coach is not here. Wade acts as both coordinator and player.

Later a few men and women are hanging around the courts. I sit on a bench complaining, "Oh gag, too stiff. Gotta get back to the machines, loosen up my squeaky joints."

Denise is standing around looking for more action. "So, some guys here say I've been invested with snake fire today. I really feel snappy. Do you wanna play a third game, Joy?"

"Uh, no, sorry, I need to drill, Denise."

"You tinned a few today. I rarely see that from you. A different game today."

"Oh, I know. I bring totally different ego involvement when I play you for a full match. A Round Robin game or two is something else."

Then my Voice-Over gets the upper hand. *"I should snap out of this and beat you like I did the other day, you cocky little 34-year-old kid."*

"Oh, well," Denise goes on, "with me, how I play depends partly on whether I feel good physically, whether I have any injuries, like my hamstring." She feels the back of her thigh.

"Yes, that too. Lots of injuries around here now."

We look at the men stretching, talking about injuries. A

short guy fingers his Achilles tendon. "I just lifted my heel to lean forwards and my heel came up, but my muscle didn't. It stuck in place. Hurts a lot, especially when I'm on the ball of my foot." Coach and this guy stretch together, focus on their physical condition and speculate as to whether the Achilles guy should play any more this week.

"Well, ice it and don't play for at least a week," counsels Coach.

"I don't understand. I stretched well before I played. I've never gotten this kind of injury before. Why did it have to happen now? A most inconvenient time."

Denise, overhearing, says, "Yeah, with me, it's my hamstring, with him, it's his tendon, with you, it's your lower back, with Tamara, it's her knee, with Mary, her knee, Pam, lower back and vertebra, Rose, her toe, Chris, just plain old sick. Let's see. Leslie—anything wrong with her?"

"Guess not."

I nod. "Uh, huh. Tamara, how's your knee?"

Tamara says, "Yeah, the guys are teasing me. I suffer from *extremis something maximus.*" She fills in the names of strained knee muscles. "Well, I gotta go now. My son's waiting for me and my knee has had enough for today. See ya."

At this Quickie Tournament fifteen men and five women are milling around the bulletin board, looking at a grid to figure out how many handicap points each player will get. Points are assessed based on level of play, age and gender. Suddenly out of the blue a woman shouts, "I get an extra point for menopause!" We hear a male voice call back, "I get an extra point for womanpause, a pause I enjoy!"

At these tournaments, it's unusual for a woman to win more than a few points beyond the ones we are given to compensate for our level of play, age, and gender. When an inexperienced woman does get a point, everyone shouts and waves their hands. When Mary Sifferman wins the Consolations based on her 12- point handicap in a game to 15, we whoop and holler. The A level guy she played looks sheepish but takes his loss well.

When Wade presents Mary with a coupon for her prize—a massage, he says straight-faced, "The massage will take place—at my house." As everyone giggles, Mary smiles and flirts back appropriately.

"No," Wade backs out, "it's at the club here, by a woman who plays squash. She's really good, at massage. Hope you enjoy it."

Denise and I look at each other, silently observing the interaction and that it is the man-woman thing, a rather rare dynamic at this club, at least among the squash players.

Doing It

Maybe. Just maybe I am getting the hang of this softball game—finally! While playing practice games with Mary, I come in under the ball and lift it up, even for drops or dribbles. That flat forceful stroke of my hardball game—it is gone. An under-over arch helps me get the best length. Sometimes I can float the ball over my opponent's head. My upper arm muscles like my new technique.

There's more. I am close to mastering a lob serve. Lob-serving a ball that arches close to the sidewall is much easier on the body than a flat hard serve. Aiming precisely is easier, too. Coach says, "Aim for the dark smudges on the front wall."

Maybe a good change in my game has developed—after a year of study and practice!

Now it seems normal to go in early before a match and prepare. I do one set of the rehab and prevention exercises. I go onto the court more flexible and get to the front more quickly for the short balls.

It is time for another test of my quest. When I call the British Columbia Squash Racquets Association (BCSRA) in Vancouver, Barbara Savage tells me about the first Masters Circuit tournament of the season. It is in Victoria.

The idea of entering this tournament I put aside for a while in order to find out whether I really want to go. The dawn of day brings ideas on how to make arrangements at work and with housing. So I call the Cedar Hill Squash Club in Victoria to get the ball rolling.

"This Masters tournament may be part of my warm-up for Nationals," I tell myself. *"Maybe each Canadian Masters Circuit tournament can keep me motivated and training for United States Nationals next year."* I don't mention my plan to anyone. Somehow I simply know this is a good move.

Training Tough

I train hard. I wear a skirt instead of shorts. I get my squash shoes repaired. There is me on the Stairmaster, sweating mightily, me doing weights conscientiously, me stretching out seriously, me asking people to play with me to help get me tournament-ready, and me concentrating hard during practice, trying to ratchet it up another notch.

One day I play a guy who drops a lot, like the women do, but he does it faster and more precisely. I scramble too much and if I get to the ball, I am not in the best control of where I put it. How can get to the front sooner? Since my major weakness is being too slow on the uptake, that is, the start-off sprint towards a front wall ball, I need to do something differently. An idea comes to me. As we play, I chant to myself:

STRIKE AND **STEP.** HIT AND **RUN.** STROKE AND **START.**
STRIKE AND **STEP.** HIT AND **RUN.** STROKE AND **START.**

Finally, after about 15 games with this guy, I get up front for his drops and short shots! Not only do I get to them, I control the front court almost as well as I control the midcourt. Finally. Slow learner.

At night I dream I am joining someone in the club restaurant for coffee, and the talk is about my training. This someone also goes with me to tournaments and is there for me as my second, my support, my prop, and my chasm-filler.

Cedar Hills Vets Tournament
Cedar Hill Squash Club
Victoria, British Columbia, Canada

The tournament takes place at Cedar Hill Municipal Recreation Centre. After undergoing a major renovation recently, the Centre has been rededicated. The squash club has an unusual partnership with this public facility. The Centre features four new wide 21-foot courts. Phil Green, the tournament director, says there are 110 entries, mostly from Vancouver Island, a few from Vancouver, and one from Seattle—me. Gray's of Cambridge is the main sponsor of this Veterans Circuit Squash tournament.

Cedar Hills Vets Tournament

My journey means that I arrive in Victoria after 9 p.m. off the Tsawwassen-Swartz Bay ferry. Although I arrive at the ferry dock on the mainland before 5:30 p.m., I have to accept a one-run wait.

Getting from the ferry dock to the Centre takes longer than it should because I get lost in the dark. My directions don't distinguish between Cedar Hill Road and Cedar Hill Crossing Road, so naturally I take the wrong road. After asking some youngsters how to get to the Centre, I arrive tired and discouraged, thinking it is too late to play. It isn't. The director gives the bedraggled me a hearty welcome.

After checking in, I call the Selkirk Guest House (the hostel) to tell them I have arrived and ask them to leave the door unlocked, since I won't be able to make it there before 11:00 p.m. When out-of-town people ask me where I am staying, I tell them about the hostel for $13.50 a night with towels and sheets. They look incredulous and say, "Why didn't I think of that?"

After changing into my playing outfit, I go onto the court for a short warm-up. The courts are a sea of faces and bodies in white and navy blue. I have brought along white shorts, a white scoop-necked top, a white headband, a fuchsia wristband, and a tight sport bra. As I expected an all-white rule, I have brought only whites. But the rule on clothing here is "Anything Goes." Some of the women wear light-colored tops and navy pleated skirts that swing capriciously when they stroke the ball. Sometimes the ball glances off their swinging pleats. When this happens, the opponent automatically gains a point or gets a handout. I am comfortable in my baggy shorts and top.

Tonight I have a problem with my heartbeat. I fear that the traveling, finding a new place in the dark, arriving late, not having time for a fast lunge-walk warm-up, and the lingering effects of four cups of coffee and not much food have left me unprepared for vigorous playing.

Game one happens quickly. Nancy Chafe and I heat up fast and sweat fast. Suddenly my heart goes bumpity bump, bumpity bump—fast and irregular. In distress at the first game's end—which I barely win, I appeal to the referee and my opponent for help. Nancy douses my neck and forehead with cold water and tells me to rest longer than the usual 90 seconds. When I feel OK—not long after—we go back on the court. I play cautiously and lose the next game, but my heartbeat stays regular.

During the last game my eye guards keep fogging up. Water that I splashed on my forehead after the fourth game drips down onto my eye guard lenses. In preparation for the match I applied anti-fog liquid to my eye guards, but the extra splashing has washed away the anti-fogger. Between points I ask the referee for extra time to re-apply this liquid. I am turned down. So I play the last game in a cataract-like cloud. I feel oblivious to anything but the black ball and the white walls. My concentration is intense. It has to be.

I am very conscious of the hurdles in this match. Somehow the points go my way. Toward the end of the match I have a chance for a point, miss it, and figure, now Nancy surges ahead. But she doesn't, she errs, and the chance to win is given back to me. I am not sure what I am listening to, but I hear something say, *"You must really want this match to go to me. It must be meant for me."* This kind of inner dialogue puts me into more determined focus and I make right decisions about placement, pace, and retrieving.

I win the match not by hitting the ball hard but by placing it at unexpected lengths. I have some lucky shots and Nancy tins some key points. My restrained exertion results in shots that drop too short for Nancy to do much with. My power game inadvertently becomes a soft touch game. Our scores are 9-7, 4-9, 10-8, and 10-9.

At the end of the match I do not feel elated, just flat. "Call the ambulance," I say to an observer, "I really wanted to lose." He grins and says, "You just keep on wanting to lose." He doesn't understand that I am worried about over-taxing my heart.

What has caused my heart problem? Was my chest bound too tightly in my new bra, making me unable to breathe enough oxygen? Was I having hot flashes combined with quick and intense exertion? I don't know, but I promise myself I will get checked out by a doctor.

On Saturday morning before my next match I am lucky to connect with a Quaker nurse. I have brought along names and phone numbers of a few Quakers from the *Traveling Friends Directory* and intended to call them just to say hello. I try one who is listed as a nurse. This Friend is home and gracious enough to talk. Upon hearing my symptoms, she advises that the coffee, exertion, and stress might have contributed to the wildly beating heart, but from what she understands about how it settled down, she thinks it is not a serious condition. Perhaps it is related to menopause. Her opinion gives me reassurance to play hard in my next match.

Trusting in my basic physical well being, I get ready for my match against Shannon McJannet from Vancouver. I review my notes about our match the previous season. Shannon is very quick, so I can't let us get into long rallies that require lots of running. So, although I don't have to rev up as much as for my Friday night match, I prepare by arriving early, stretching well, and making certain my equipment, hair, clothing, and towel are in good order. I go outdoors for a walk and do a fast bent-knee walk around the tennis courts. I avoid the squash area so as not to overburden my senses and stiffen up. Then, inside I ride a stationary bike for a while.

Playing smartly and calmly, I do my new sidearm serves. They are tight to the wall. I do some hard drive serves, too. Shannon is nervous and her serves are not good. She seems weak, although she is very fit. She makes some errors and the score is a quick 3-0.

During this match I feel better than I did the night before. I focus well and get in some good serves, so we don't have many long rallies. My pulse stays steady.

Later Shannon says, "I hope you play in the A's now."

"Really?" I reply, "Why?"

"Your serves, your drives, your crosscourts, the speed of your shots—they are all too much for us in the B's."

"But," I contend, "I can't move from back to front except sometimes."

"Well, you're much better than the last time we played."

"Well, if I play A's, I won't have any chance to win."

"Sometimes, the A category is divided into two draws, Open and low A's. You could fit into low A's. But I guess, if you're still getting good matches in the B's, stay in B's."

"We'll see, after tomorrow. In Seattle I don't win the B's, but those tournaments are not age group only. In them I have to play against women in their twenties and thirties."

Later, one of the fellows who saw my Friday match asks me if I am in the Finals. "Yes," I say.

"Great. I saw your match last night. Uhhhh!" He punches the air with his fist in approving emphasis.

"That match was weird," I acknowledge.

This guy is in the Men's A Final, so I feel reinforced by his attention.

The next day finds me still feeling fine. My opponent in the Finals is Marg Hepper. At age 51 she has great legs, and definitely looks under 50. She arrives 15 minutes before match time.

Again I am wearing my old white shorts with the elastic waistband. I have brought skirts, but feel it would be poor taste to run around in a short skirt at my age with my legs. Besides, my skirts are a little tight at the waist and don't give way while I am exerting.

At first, Marg's hard serves to my backhand throw me off. I drop the first four points on poor service returns. Marg is awarded four strokes because I don't clear to the T after my forehand rails. After settling in, I play carefully as well as adventurously and wait for my opponent's inconsistency to show.

In our last game Marg errs out, while I hinge it up. Because I don't hit as hard off the back wall as Marg wants, the length of my drives bothers her and I put away her returns. I win 3-2 to win the Women's B draw. Games scores are something like 4-9, 9-2, 5-9, 9-7, 9-3. When we finish our fifth game, I frisbee my racquet onto the court's floor in relief. Then I pick it up, shake hands with my opponent, say thank you to the referee, walk off the court, and shake hands with three fans, including Shannon.

Later I learn that Marg partied all night until 7:30 in the morning. She claims it was worth it, even though she lost in the Finals, because she had a good time at her reunion.

After our match a young woman in the C-D draw comments on my focus. She notices that I arrive early and prepare myself. This player has a slightly admiring countenance and tone. Could it be that I might get, might someday deserve, admiration on the squash court similar to what has come so easily from my students? For me the squash court is a harder place to shine than the classroom.

To my amazement some people have noticed my presence at these tournaments. For instance, Shannon planned to travel over to Victoria from Vancouver with a girl friend, but her friend withdrew after injuring her leg, so Shannon had to decide whether to travel to this tournament solo or withdraw. Her husband and kids don't play squash. In deciding whether to go by herself, she concluded, "That lady from Seattle does it, so, so can I."

On Sunday when I return some towels to the hostel's hostess, I tell her that I won the Women's B draw. She gives me a big hug and we exchange squash talk. She used to play.

In the hostel I see Bahai materials. I talk with the hostess about the kinship between Bahai and Quakerism. Whimsically, I sign her guest book, feeling like a minor celebrity.

I leave Vancouver Island richer in spirit, motivation, and knowledge about how to do an out-of-town tournament. Proudly I put my stuff into my new squash bag— my prize for winning my age-group draw. It is tastefully garnished with gold lettering "Gray's of Cambridge," and I like it much better than the garish sport bags I have seen in Seattle.

One pleasant consequence of this competing is the sight of my belly as I bend over while changing clothes. My protruding fat belly is minus a wad. My diet of Power Bars, apples, and water, supplemented by Mari Lu crackers, is a factor. Will I gain the belly back next week? Will I ever stop worrying about it?

At home Rob and I celebrate in our usual way—talking, cuddling, and lovemaking. I continue to train, this time consistently. One night, knowing I have to play early the next morning, I turn Rob down. I tell him why. He accepts my decision. "Gotta do what you gotta do. Go for it!"

Arbutus Vets Tournament
The Arbutus Club
Vancouver, British Columbia, Canada

For the next tournament I am psyched. Driving north to Vancouver, I sing and move to the beat of the audiotape *"Cool Runnings."* My mind's eye keeps a clear picture of those determined Jamaican bobsled athletes, training idealistically and fixating on their goals. *"Keep your eyes on the prize, put them a little bit higher."*

Those guys in the movie went to Calgary, Alberta, to train. I am going to places in British Columbia. These Vets tournaments are as close as I will ever get to any Olympic Trials.

The Arbutus Club is in a pleasant neighborhood. The building is suited for multi-purpose sports. I arrive in plenty of time, walk in with my sport bag and racquet, and follow the signs to the squash courts. I check in at the tournament desk, get tournament information and tickets for beer. I look around for the locker room and find one filled with girls.

"Are there hair dryers?" I ask.

"Oh, there might be in the Women's change room."

"Oh, this is not for women?"

Court Quest

"No, next one down."

I sigh, "But the sign says, 'Women and Girls.'"

The next door opens into a small room. Only one person is in it, a woman in a wet swimsuit. I overhear her talking with a friend:

"How've you been?"

"Oh, I've been not well, in hospital."

"Oh? Sorry! What was it...?"

"Nerves, kind of a breakdown. I'm separating from my husband."

"Oh, sorry to hear that."

"That's why this feels so good, to swim, to calm down."

This room doesn't appear to have any lockers, so I go looking for another. I carry my stuff through a fancy glass door marked by the word "Push." I glance around at a nice foyer with carpets, flowers, mirrors, a sofa, and a man using the telephone. He turns and says to me, "Oh, this is the Men's!"

I stop, "Oh, gag—."

He smiles and says, "You can go on in, if you wish," waving his hand towards the next door.

I mutter a no thanks as he says, "Go out the other door, and push on it. It enters into the Ladies' shower room."

"Thanks." I feel relief and start to chuckle.

In the Women's change room, I put my stuff into a locker and secure it with my lock and key. I go to the washroom. I return to the lockers and stop in front of one that looks exactly like the one I placed my lock on. I put my key in the lock, fumble with it, and frown. A woman in a towel arrives and looks puzzled at seeing me fiddling with that lock. Instantly I register what I have done, shrug my shoulders in exasperation, and move on to the next carrel of lockers. "What a bumbler," I chuckle.

Later, all ready to play, I head for the exit door. I look down at my shoes; my shoelaces are loose. I put my leather racquet case and a towel on something beneath some shelves stacked with towels. As I bend to adjust my shoelaces, I hear a clank as the racquet and towel fall from sight. "Oh, my God. The laundry chute! My racquet— the basement!" I spy a cabinet door below the shelf on which I placed my stuff, open it, and see my racquet and towel on a glob of used wet towels. I sigh again and smirk widely. Pulling my stuff out and clutching my racquet to my body, I open an unmarked door and go searching for the courts. I caution myself: "It would be really cool if I owned a back-up racquet."

In the weight room and on a racquetball court I do a pre-match routine. My preparation is ten minutes on the stationary bike, one set of push-downs, ten minutes of stretching, and five minutes running patterns.

My food two hours before match time is a Power Bar, a can of V-8 juice, and water. It is enough.

I am curious about court clothing. What I don't bring is what several women are wearing—a light pink pleated skirt. My pink is hot pink knee length Lycra tights!

"What is the dress code?" I ask the tournament director. "I brought shorts, a skirt, and these things that come over the knee. I could wear a long shirt over them." I pantomime putting on a long T-shirt over my tights.

"We are not all-white. You can wear pretty much what you want."

"I guess my tights are Lycra."

"We prefer not Lycra. Under your shorts, all right, but we prefer not Lycra only."

"Oh, they are so nice."

"But if that's the only thing you brought—."

"Oh no, I brought everything, but I like the Lycra. They keep the muscles warm."

"Yes, practice in them."

In the end I wear white shorts over the hot pink Lycra tights.

My draw is Levels A and B combined. My new skills show up on the court. I go five games with Ann Wittsel, an experienced and younger A player. In the first game I give away the first four points, as usual. I am erratic, nervous, and uncoordinated. After losing two games, I try new approaches and win two games. Before the fifth game I try self-talk and quick meditation. The round white light appears in my mind's eye. I mind-talk, *"My body is running perfectly. It can do anything gracefully."* Then onto the court I walk and win several put-away shots from the front court. But in the end Wittsel edges me out.

After my first match I return to the Women's change room. I undress, secure my lock to a locker and take two towels with me to the showers. When I return, I put my key in the lock, open the door, and see it is empty! "What?" Instantly I spy the adjacent locker on which there is *no* lock. I open it and see my stuff inside. Breathing a sigh of relief, I chuckle again.

I hear one player ask another how she is playing. "Not as well as I want to. Lost my drive. Made too many errors in the last games. Not fit enough, I guess."

I speak up, "Well, I can't help overhearing, and I don't think I'm prying, but I always ask myself what time of my cycle it is. There are certain times I play better."

"Oh, interesting. Actually, I just started. I'm in it." Our

Arbutus Vets Tournament

eyes register understanding.

Later I hear this woman talking with someone about politics: "I don't know about you, but I know for certain I will never vote for a woman prime minister until she's on the other side of her monthly up and down, you know what I mean? That emotional roller coaster. I'll wait until she's beyond it."

The other woman says, "I agree. If she's anything like me...."

My next match goes five games, also. I win against another Ann—Ann Paris. Scores are 10-8, 8-10, 5-9, 9-2, 9-4. I hear that this is Ann's first tournament of the season, so I deduce that she is vulnerable to pressure, pace, and speed.

Ann Paris is 56 years old, medium height, medium build and left-handed. She moves well, especially when she has to turn in a different direction. Her best shot is a forehand kill drive from the red mid-court line. If her opponent's hard serve is low, she returns a drop two-wall shot. She covers the back court well, preferring a two-wall drop to end a rally. Her lob serve to my backhand comes high.

I prevail by scrambling for short returns and doing drop defensive returns. We have only one stroke and only a couple of lets. Several of my serves are high. In game two I am up 7-2, lose concentration, and lose this game.

We have fairly equivalent skills and court sense. "It's all mental at this age," says Ann. During the fifth game she loses concentration and makes some unforced errors, handing the win to me.

To round out this tournament, I have the privilege of watching Joyce Maycock play. For the first time Joyce, the Women's World 40-Plus champion, plays in the 45-Plus age group. No woman at this tournament can give her a good match, so she plays Men's A. After a slow start, Maycock plays well, gets better as the match progresses, and wins decisively with a series of precise, unexpected kill shots and gets. Between games she isn't even winded.

Age, Sport Bras, Head Bands, and Kids

Back in Seattle, I am playing a big man who doesn't like to run. I play fairly well and get a game off him. By the last game I am bending, reaching, and running better. Mr. Big Man gets sloppier.

Squash buddy Terry asks me about the Canadian tournament I just played.

"The women you played, were they all 45-Plus B?"

"It was combined A and B."

"Were they all good?"

"Some, not all."

Mr. Big Man walks up, all sweaty and toweling off. "I heard you say you were in the 50-Plus age group. Are you that old?"

"Yes. I'm fifty-and-a-half."

"Man, I thought you were *younger* than me and I'm 46." He gives a noise that sounds like, "And I let you get a game off me!"

Later in the club restaurant a guy asks me, "How did you do against Mr. Big Man?"

"Oh, OK. Actually got a game, but I didn't get him very worried in other games. Too slow, I guess."

"Oh?"

"But I made him run."

"Great. Anybody who can make him run is—he just leans and stabs at the ball."

"Yeah, an octopus."

In the locker room Tamara is trying to wiggle out of her

Age, Sport Bras, Head Bands and Kids

sport bra.

"Now I know how my grandmother felt when she wore her corset."

"Uh huh, me, too," I sympathize.

"I bought a new sport bra and it's so tight, it's killing me. I can't get it on and off. There's no clasp."

"Oh dear," I nod.

"This afternoon, trying to get this thing on, I think I strained a muscle in my forearm."

"Uh, huh." I can't help laughing.

"No way to undo it, and it flattens me down, and I'm already flat!"

"Oh dear."

"Actually, I bought another one recently. It has a clasp and two shaped cups. Expensive, though."

"Yup. Let's invent something better–better and cheaper."

"Yeah, something that doesn't show everything when you sweat."

"It doesn't matter what you wear underneath, anyway. When you sweat, especially in this weather, it's like wearing an instantly wet T-shirt. I hope folks understand we're not going Form Fit deliberately."

"What I'd like is a T-shirt fabric like cotton candy, that kinda hangs out from your bra in a puff while you're playing, but doesn't get in the way of a passing ball."

"Yeah, let's invent it. All the squash clothes are made with men in mind anyway. Why not invent a bra exclusively for women who play squash? One that automatically flattens your breasts when you coil up for a backhand drive."

"Good idea, Joy. They do get in the way."

Later some of us are sitting on a bench watching Coach

give a lesson.

"I'm waiting for her lesson to be finished, so I can have my lesson," says Denise.

Tamara says, "He's dating her. I was at a party where he brought her. She's nice."

"Really? How old is she? I bet Coach wishes he hadn't lost so much of his hair," says Denise.

"And it is still disappearing, as we speak," observes Tamara.

I pipe up, "I don't know. He looks kinda cute with it gone like that."

"I guess it's the head band," ventures Tamara. "Looks like a vegetable strainer without the strainer part."

A Little Lesson

I am eager for my monthly mini-lesson. It comes with the membership.

"What would you like to work on?" Coach asks.

"Well, what do you think I need to work on?"

"Well, your backhand is still your weakest. Go ahead, hit some backhands, some rails."

Plop, plop, plop, I hit the ball. Coach makes some good points. I am trying to keep my elbow too close to my body. I need to let my arm swing like a pendulum— pooch the elbow out on the back swing, follow through with arm up, elbow bent a little. In the set up, I should conform the racquet and arm to form the letter "U."

I shake my head slightly as I absorb his advice. Drowning out his words are sounds on the next court. Some one is drilling by himself. I love the sound of squash balls plopping against the front wall in a steady, rhythmical pattern.

Competitive Dynamics

One evening I walk into the court area and see Coach and Denise doing a lesson.

Later Denise and I are warming up to play.

"You made it back, Joy. Where'd you go?"

"Ski Star."

"How was it?"

"Great. The place wasn't open for the season yet, so I parked for free. Some trails were already packed down. Some were not. I saw maybe five people, lots of sun and dry snow."

Denise is crestfallen. "I wish I had gone with you. Fresh air. I can see it in your cheeks."

"How was your lesson?"

She looks pained. "OK. He got into my basic shot, my form, again. He does that about every three or four weeks."

"Distressing."

We play hard, have few unforced errors, and switch from Denise dominating to me dominating. Gradually Denise loses focus, will, and strength— typical for her after a long lesson.

After playing, Denise takes off and I stick around to stretch out slowly and warm down. Two guys are playing an intense game.

The receiver hits the tin. "Shit!" he says.

The other guy serves, saying nothing.

The receiver mishits the ball again and loses the point. "You bag of dirt! You shithead!"

The server says the score, "6-2," and then serves.

The receiver hits the serve out. "Fuck!"

The server looks at me, stares at his opponent, and then looks back at me. He serves again.

The receiver misses the ball. "Darn. Move your butt!"

I smile at the linguistic change. "I hope I'm never that down on myself and my game," I muse.

The Nutritionist

I keep my appointment with Janet, the club's nutritionist.

"So, what did you eat before your match today?"

"A cup of chili, a piece of apple pie with cinnamon sauce, and two glasses of hot spiced cider."

"Sounds pretty good. How was your energy level? Any lightheadedness?"

"High energy. Felt strong."

"What for breakfast before you went skiing?"

"A peanut butter and honey sandwich, a glass of milk made from non-fat organic milk powder."

"Good. I'll note that on your chart. Come in again next week with a detailed list of what you ate on days you exercised vigorously. OK?"

"Right. Thanks a lot."

"One more question. You said last time that you felt uncoordinated, bloated, and mentally off after you used the estrogen vaginally three times in a week. Are you still using the estrogen?"

"Nope. Don't intend to again. Got really turned on sexually. That was great. But then my period was so scanty. It was like it started but got confused and didn't do a complete job. Then a few days later I had some spotting. That makes me nervous, and I'm always worrying that the red stuff is an indication of uterine cancer. Pooh on it. No more for me."

"Well, you are still making estrogen in your fat cells,

remember. As long as you have extra fat on your body, you probably have enough estrogen in your system to make an effect on how you function and how you feel."

"I know that, I guess. I just thought it was time to try it. I hadn't had a period in a couple of months and was beginning to feel mighty uninterested."

"I understand."

"You do? I bet you don't, really. You're such a baby."

"Imagination doesn't count here?"

"Not in my book. You just wait. Maybe by that time they'll have something better for menopausal women, something estrogen-like without the side effects."

'I hope so! Bye for now!"

Which Tournament and When?

Hilary and I plunk our squash bags on the carpet next to our table in the club's cafe. We order pineapple juice.

"Joy, are you gonna enter the downtown tournament?"

"I dunno yet. You?"

"I kinda want to, but I'm not playing enough."

"Well, I'm playing enough, but I wonder if they'll have age-group draws.

I glance at a copy of the United States Squash Racquets Association newsletter. "It says here that the date of the next National Softball tournament might be moved."

"Yeah? To what?"

"Maybe April. A lot of people have complained about its being held in September. That time has always seemed awkward to me, too. Just when folks around here are coming off the water, still entranced with our few weeks of summer and still craving to do something outdoors, we have to come inside and train for Nationals?"

"Exactly. Hiking. Biking. Swimming in cool mountain lakes."

"The entries are already out for the next World Masters Tournament."

"When is it?"

"Fall of next year."

"You planning to go?"

"To Australia?"

"Wouldn't that be great?"

"Yeah, I think you should go. Give that woman a run for her money. Make her sweat."

"You mean Goldie Edwards?"

"Uh huh."

"It says here on another page that Joyce Davenport won it, Women's 50-Plus, at the '93 U. S. Nationals in San Francisco. She gave up just two points!"

"Hum. I wonder why Goldie didn't enter. Maybe she retired? Was injured? I thought she'd last forever."

"Like Heather McKay. I read someplace where she won the World's Masters 50-Plus in Scotland recently. No competition really."

"You know, it's too bad Heather hasn't gotten the recognition she deserves. All those decades of being the number one woman squash player in the world, and she has little fame."

"I hope the people close to Heather give her the accolades she deserves. Certainly the media and the masses in the USA don't have a clue as to what a great athlete she is."

"I wonder how long she'll play."

"Me too. Apparently, the oldest player in U. S. Nationals this year was an 87 year-old man. The oldest woman was

67. So, Joy, you want to be the first woman to be playing squash at age 100, huh?"

"Yeah, how'd you guess?"

"Well, you'd better get down there and start drilling some shots. Wouldn't want you to get rusty sitting around."

""OK, OK, Coach, I hear you." I giggle.

"I gotta go. See you next week?"

"I hope so. I mean, sure, you betcha!" I grin.

More Training

In the weight room I move from Cybex machine to Cybex machine and then to free weights. I carry my weight-training card and a pencil with me. Nearby is a towel I can drape over a bench dotted with sweat from a previous user. A mixture of men and women, young and not young, inhabit the weight room. My outfit for this workout is a long, loose T-shirt and black Lycra tights. Others in the weight room are wearing more body-revealing outfits.

"How many sets do I feel like doing today? Oh, one set, I guess, but 13 or 14 reps instead of 12. Do the settings my trainer decided on for me."

My breathing is audible: In, out, in, out. My trainer says to exhale on the push, inhale on the rest.

It is nice that this trainer says I look good for 50, but more important is the question: will Cybex workouts, massage, and free weights do anything to diminish night sweats and warm flashes? When I look with a flushed magenta face at these hunky males in the weight room, it is not because they have aroused my sexual fantasies. It is because my temperature center has gone wacko.

I am amused at the phenomenon that propels men and

Court Quest

women into the gym to focus on body sculpting. They don't do a sport—just weights. Many of them have fallen for the advertising that the more muscular they are, the more likely they will meet the mate of their dreams, maybe someone also into body sculpting. Many men and women are obsessed with their percentage of lean body mass. Body image is in. Personality development is out.

The aerobics class promises beauty and fitness. It is full of people doing extraordinary physical and musical things. Rectangular rubber step-benches capture us. Around, beside, and on them we have to prance. Two or three of these step-benches stacked on top of each other bring misery to my calves and knees, so I do the patterns without a step-bench.

I watch the exercisers copying Jimmie's gyrations. They do well at imitating his intricate movements. I watch, try, and mess up. Even the throbbing, blaring beat of the cassette tape can't help me do the footwork on time. I am usually a half a beat slow. During warm-down I make a feeble attempt at doing the final push-ups and contortionist stretching and then decide this is not the class for me.

Later I go into the fitness room and place myself on the last empty treadmill. A woman next to me is running vigorously at seven miles per hour. *"If she can do that speed, so can I."*

I push some buttons on the treadmill to get going at three mph, which is only a fast walking speed. I speak to the woman next to me. "Didn't you just do an hour of Jimmie's aerobics class?"

Miss Vigor answers, "Uh huh" and nods.

"Uh, I hope you don't mind if I ask, but wasn't that class enough? What are you training for?"

"Nothing special. I just like to get really tired. It's too dark and rainy to run outside nowadays."

"Do you compete in anything?"

"Nope, not interested. Just like doing this. Makes me feel good."

"So, how much time do you spend working out every day?"

"A couple of hours, except Saturday. Then I come in twice for three hours altogether."

"You say you're not in training for anything special?"

"Nope." Big pause. "Well, OK, it's only fair to tell you. My boyfriend works here. Lots of hours, too, so it's one way to see some of him during the day."

"Oh. Uh huh."

"Why am I disappointed by this information?"

Crisis

I am in trouble at work. A misunderstanding by a suspicious colleague means that my best December energy has to go into defending myself to prevent a permanent blight on my record. I rally my faculty union representatives to help me.

During the reprimand process my mind and character function bravely. But my emotions freeze on anger that cascades into my muscles and makes me sprawl on my futon and blank out the world.

One consequence of my crisis is that I am unable to focus on anything but continuing to teach my classes and resolving the crisis. I withdraw from the December Vets Tournament in Canada as well as the December in-house tournament. This Vets tournament is the one I vowed the year before to return to and win—in my age group.

Being thwarted by more-powerful-than-me-forces is not pleasant. I feel hopeless about improving the circumstances under which I work. Rob empathizes with me, as he has had his share of problems in his department and understands the politics of a college. "The thing to do is be cool. Don't let them know they are getting to you. Kill them with kindness."

Doldrums

For a few weeks after resolution of the problem in my favor, I react by staying in social and athletic isolation. Between school terms I don't have to go anyplace, so I don't. My son doesn't come home from Rhode Island for the holidays. Rob leaves, as usual, so my solitude, if I want it, can be total.

I assess my mind and emotions. How down do I feel, really? I have to go back to work, but I don't have to do much else. Will I go back to squash? Will I go back to training? Do I care about squash anymore? How can I change my job, my life?

I don't want to go back there and teach. At work I function on at least two tracks, as I do in my personal life: one track reflects clarity, cheerfulness, efficiency, graciousness, and industriousness. Simultaneously, *Sturm und Drang* beset me. I am still looking for personal contentment and satisfactory employment.

The days are dark, cold, and sloppy. Nobody calls me. I sleep a lot, watch television, and read two books: *Gilgamesh the King* by Robert Silverberg and *House of Spirits* by Isabel Allende.

I avoid anybody and any activity. I do not eat much, do not clean the house at all. My mood is zombie-like, but in

Doldrums

a way, peaceful.

It isn't hard to get in the mode of doing nothing physical. Being sedentary feels pleasant, and I am seduced into thinking that lolling around could be pleasant for a long time. I lapse into doing nothing and wonder, if I carry on like this, how much mind-spirit stuff I will get into.

Then the downside starts—-the lower back awareness, the skin eruptions, the puffy cheeks, the flabbier torso, the dull eyes, the unpropped-up voice, and the low spirits. I muse and brood. The world has so much violence. My problems seem large. I see only obstacles ahead.

Evaluating my circumstances, I toy with giving up squash altogether. Is this the time to pull out of my quest? Should I chuck my goals, the hours of practice, the effort to understand and improve my game? Should I save myself the stress of traveling alone to another country in rotten weather?

I could use the money I spend on sport for paying bills. I could save a lot by simply running, walking, and cross-country skiing. Unfortunately, because my position at the college is secure, even though I am unhappy there, I am not motivated enough to look seriously for a change.

Sometimes I skim the Help Wanted ads for other jobs and job training. What I could do or learn to do quickly seems boring and stultifying. Entry-level pay or a little above is meager. I am shocked at how meager.

One attractive job is truck driver. I could get out of town. But driving would take me away from Rob. Being with him recently has perked me up a bit. He is a big blip of up, a cheerful churning that propels me into my regular self. He is good at not letting things get to him, good at chiding me into seeing the brighter side of things.

Court Quest

Days pass. At last something changes within me. I take down the Christmas lights, feel the Chinook wind's warmth, and gaze at my pussywillow tree's catkins.

I drive to the club, willing to do something mildly energetic. When I get into a water aerobics class, I feel surprised at its slow pace. It does not do much for me. It is geared to older and unfit people.

It is a good day to walk into the club. People at the front desk notice I have not been around for a while. Someone comments on my win at the Cedar Hill Vets tournament. By now the results have been printed in a squash newsletter.

I run into some women taking lessons. They are cheerful. Sensing that I am dipping, Tamara says, "I always say— one's capacity to feel pain is equal to one's capacity to feel love and joy."

"Thanks a lot, Tamara."

Someone else mentions the Vancouver tournament, and Tamara says, "Yes, she's the scourge of Canada. They run when she goes up for a tournament."

This comment is strangely discomforting and also welcome. I hit by myself and judge that doing so feels good. Then I do a full routine of weights. This also feels good.

How much my mood is colored by my dread of going back to work and starting a new quarter of teaching, I don't know. I have to be on guard. I have been warned to toe the line, not ruffle any feathers.

I wonder if I will be able to muster the courage and the oomph to fight once more against the unfair treatment dished out to less-than-full-time faculty. Imagining other possible work, I lean towards solitary things such as court reporter— where there is simply the job to do and no people to organize.

Doldrums

In desperation, I take a popular occupational preference test through the college counseling office. My results indicate that my first choice of occupation, what I am most suited for, is teaching.

One day during my gloom a dream comes to me and stays:

She is in bed, her arms wrapped around herself. A hot water bottle wrapped in a flannel pillowcase is draped over her bare feet. She looks at the clock. It is too early, 5:30 a.m. She throws off the quilt, changes position, and puts her hand down to feel her most unfavorite wad of fat, her belly.

"I'll never get rid of this. It's slowing me down. Soon I'll look like a straight tube of rubber blubber."

She rolls tighter into a fetal ball. She hides her face under the sheet and dozes. "I am not getting up until I absolutely have to."

She doze-dreams about squash balls flying around a court, slow and black, interspersed with faces of immigrant students, hopeful students, cheerful, eager, some formerly tortured refugee students, gold teeth in big smiles, missing teeth in small smiles. She faces them bravely, ministering unto them with gestures, silent talking and crisp enunciation, while the warmth of everyone's caring fills the room.

The cold silent white squash courts are empty except for her and her racquet. The dark green ball punctuated by a yellow dot drops and plops. She drills a mishmash of good shots, hopeless shots, and bloopy shots.

The telephone rings. I reach out to answer it and force myself to sit up on the bed, thinking, "The least I can do for my dignity is to be up and moving."

"Hello?"

"Huh, you sound like you're still in bed," says a deep male voice I recognize.

"I am. I'm depressed."
"Why?"
"You. Oh, I don't know."
"You're not sick."
"Uh huh."
"You don't have cancer."
"Uh huh."
"You have a job to go to."
"Then it's nothing to be depressed about."
"I'm staying here until you get here."
"That's why I called. To tell you I'll be in at 1:30. Can you pick me up though?"
"Sure. Where."
"The usual place."
OK. See ya. 1:30."
"Bye bye."

I fall back onto the bed. I hear the garbage truck on its way to pick up recyclables. I throw on some old clothes, place the recycle bin on the parking strip, and return inside. I check the time and contemplate whether I am awake enough to stay up. Suddenly, I shutter my shoulders back and gather up my squash bag.

A Lift

At the club people look at me as though I have had a hard night. They seem easy on me, almost apologetic. Women are solicitous, offering to hit with me after they finish their lessons.

On the court I drill solo. I have visions of myself on the court having a lesson. Then dollar signs splatter the walls. I shake my head. I have to practice by myself.

A Lift

Alone on the court, I do a good serve and then step to the T. Peeking through the glass back wall, Coach observes me. I sense him, turn, and acknowledge him. He smiles and postures to speak.

"That was a better serve, easier to get to the T than the other serve you do."

"Yes, I'm trying it."

"You are going up in the front of the T now."

"Yes, because those women in Canada, they return the serve short and low. I tend to stay back behind the red line."

"Well, that's all right. See here, the T where the red line is faded, that's where most people stand."

"Uh huh. But if you are playing women and they hit short?"

"Then you have to move up."

I try moving up, bending my knees a lot.

"Don't bend your knees too much. It's harder to move."

I correct my knee position and smile at him.

He smiles back, his eyes light up a little; then he turns toward the other court and drifts away.

"Thanks."

"Huh."

I go to the locker room and change into a swimsuit. I get into the pool and swim laps hard, executing good flip turns. Nearby, I see a water aerobics class filled with old people splashing around.

My Voice-Over takes over: *"By your age in years you should be over there with them. No, no, no. Remember your VO2 score was off the chart. Remember, you can do it. Your body is just waiting for you to train it, so it can perform beautifully for you. Just waiting."*

Back in the locker room I change into a warm-up suit. I

put my swimsuit, cap, and goggles in a sink of water and sprinkle anti-chlorine powder on them. I exit the club, leaving my stuff in the sink. When I get home and go to hang up my suit, I realize what I have done. I call the club and they fetch my stuff.

"Again! Again I left something someplace! That's the third time this week! What is going on? Menopausal memory loss?"

I sit and think some more.

"All right, so you went down to the bus company and filled out a form for training as a tour bus driver and tour guide. You didn't think ahead enough to realize that the diesel fumes would kill your lungs, your great and wonderful VO2 lungs. So you are blue about not finding another job right away, after only your first foray out there."

"Silly woman, don't you know that you are your own best investment? Don't look at a company. Invest in yourself. You have yourself and your gifts to offer. Don't get distracted. Keep your sense on the racquet's sweet spot. Your lifeline is the magic spot six inches below the high red line on the court. Your serve will serve you well."

Something Beckoning

It is time to press dreams to the side. My mode becomes analytical. I organize my life and get my home office in order. Things are too messy, too disorganized. I decide to get back to the discipline of setting goals and going for them.

The squash scene is beckoning. I have only to get to it.

I decide to have another fitness evaluation. My blood pressure registers 102 over 60. Pulse is 62. VO2 score is amazing, off the chart again for my age. My weight the trainer knows, but I don't, because I always close my eyes when I step on a scale. The trainer does a body fat percentage measurement by the caliper method. She estimates between 20 and 30% body fat. Lean and mean is the fashion, 12-15% fat for women. I am fit though still fat.

I am worried about Rob. Now that winter term classes have started, things are stable, even though he is very worried about his contract not being renewed for the following year because of his age and health problems. About this eventuality I can do nothing. I regret it for him deeply though, since he still loves teaching and the life of teaching and doesn't want to be forced into retirement.

For myself, to perk myself up, I can go outside into daylight. I can walk through the neighborhood, searching for pussywillows. I can run around the running track in the dewy morning.

At night after a mini-lesson I play some squash. I practice deep crosscourt drives. Squash is stabilizing.

My menses comes. I wonder at it and wonder if I have been holding stress down, avoiding extra physical stress in an effort to help my body do a normal cycle and not spot weirdly. Coming in at three weeks is within normal, I have been told. So in relief I am mentally up again.

At work I have three very full classes to teach and so far this quarter I have not tripped over my mouth. My energy stays high.

One night during a game with Tamara, after decent stretching and a regular court warm-up, while I am running after the ball, my heartbeat gets too fast for a few seconds. Then between serves it settles into a proper pace. I mention this fluttering to Tamara. "Sometimes I feel something similar and I'm quite a bit younger than you."

Is it relevant that recently I have had drenching night-sweats? They are the best: wet-nightgown-wake-you-up-throw-it-off-you-night-sweats.

West Coast Vets Tournament
Nanaimo Squash Club
Nanaimo, Vancouver Island,
British Columbia, Canada

The sun is out, glistening snow on mountains surrounds Vancouver. The world is gorgeous.

On the upper deck of the ferry to Nanaimo I find a new penny. I ask someone to take my picture with my camera and he does.

I am not sure where I am headed or how to get there. I left at home the piece of paper on which I had drawn a map to Nanaimo Squash Club and the Bed and Breakfast where I am staying. Also, I left the red entry form with the club's phone number and address. Wisely, I ate a fried egg sandwich for breakfast and have brought snack food.

I buy lunch on the ferry and it turns out to be a very good beef barley soup. My goal is to get to the club early enough with enough food and no caffeine in me to do a decent warm-up, some stretching, and the match without feeling strange.

I get to the club by 3:30 p.m., talk to the Club Pro Bob Ballinger, and agree to play at 6:00 p.m. rather than at 10:00 p.m. A spot has opened up because a player had to withdraw from the tournament. Playing earlier is fine with me, although I wonder whether my lunch will be fully digested by that time. There are only four courts, so some matches have to start as late as 11:00 p.m.

When I see the name "Nancy" on the draw sheet, I look in my notebook and read that I played a Nancy in Victoria the night my heartbeat got so irregular. I don't want to play that Nancy again. I am not ready to fight so ferociously again and risk another heart episode. But this match is with a different Nancy, Nancy Stern, seeded number one, therefore the best in the draw. I will have little chance to win, no matter how ferociously I play. My goal becomes to play well and rise to the occasion. I am relieved that Mariza from the Seattle Club is not here.

I lose to Nancy 3-0 and enjoy it. Nancy does a shot I want to master—a high three-wall for a winner, especially off a serve to her forehand. Nancy also likes to hit a backhand three-wall from deep, a shot I don't read fast enough to move on. On these courts the ball stays up relatively long, so Nancy is able to get to my drops. Basically, she gets me into the backcourt and puts away my weak defensive returns. Our scores are 9-4, 9-7, 9-0. Seven points in a game are the most anyone gets off Nancy in this tournament.

Stern is 35 and ranked number 18 in Canada. She is also the mother of a ten year-old boy whose rooting for her during our match includes a lot of noise. After the first game she discreetly puts a stop to it.

I have no heart palpitations, only a brief very fast uptick in the beating speed after a hard serve and long rally.

This tournament is the first time I have watched women's matches in the 35-Plus A/Open draw. Previously, I have been preoccupied with self-preparation and the B level players. These A/Open women are fighters and they are good. I look at my name in the A draw and sigh.

The women are aggressive, determined, fast, smart, fairly consistent, and willing to argue with the officials about lets and strokes. They don't give up. They hit hard—maybe too hard for these hot courts. They serve hard, but they don't vary their serves much. They have good anticipation at the front and get most of the three-walls, partly because they are standing in the fluid T. I am the oldest woman competing.

The men seem a little older, chubbier, and less athletic looking than the ones I have noticed at other Vets tournaments. Our interaction is mainly a glance, no conversation. Sometimes the pleasantries of chatting open up, if I am amenable to them. Most often I am not. Deep down, I am always with Rob, especially now that I foresee when we will be split apart.

In the locker room I take my time quietly. Strange voices are speaking.

"I hope they don't have a dress code here. I brought black shorts."

"Not here."

"Oh, I ate too late. My stomach's full still, but I have to eat. I'd rather have it too full than too empty."

When I hear two women prancing and singing into the locker room, I smile. One of them is Nancy Stern. It pleases me that such a serious player is cheerful. She asks me, "Who are you playing in the Consolation Finals?"

"Sylvia."

"Oh, she's pretty good."

Nancy looks at me, senses something, smiles, and adds, "But so are you."

Of course, I smile back gratefully. I feel like a groupie, hanging on to Nancy's every word and gesture.

I am sure I haven't lost weight during this tournament, but certainly my energy is sustained. I could play hours more. Of my three matches only the last one goes more than three games. My second match against Sharon Stafford is mine 3-0. The Consolation Finals I lose 3-1 to a very quick Sylvia Strosel.

I have done a few things right, showing that I am learning how to do tournaments. I get there on time and in daylight. I bring towels and a lock. I attach a safety pin to my locker key and pin the key to my shorts. I become familiar with the club's layout, including the locker room and the drinking fountain. Before match time I hit on the court to get familiar with the lighting, sounds, bounce, temperature, court size, wall color, the tin and its distracting advertisements, the door, and its handle. I warm up by stretching and doing a few minutes on a treadmill set to a highly elevated slope. Unfortunately, I do not anticipate how much the courts heat up as play progresses. In the basement of a concrete building, the courts have neither fans nor air-conditioning. Had I anticipated the heat, I would have brought some lighter weight clothing, akin to Nancy's summer weight paisley print outfit. Little by little—details.

Goodwill abounds at the awards dinner. Bob Ballinger, new Head Pro and too young to enter the Vets tournaments, jokes that he has learned a lot about Vets competitions. For instance, it is acceptable to take as much time as you want between points. You can even kick the ball to a wall and walk slowly to get it.

During the commentary, I am recognized as the sole international entry. I stand and wave to applause.

Someone says I have masterful shots, but am slow. What to do about this fact? Nothing. Twenty pounds and twenty years are insurmountable.

I joke to Sylvia: "I have 50 more years to play. I intend to be a pioneering woman at Regionals, Nationals, and Worlds. I want to be an example to officials who are observing the need to add another five-year age bracket to the Women's draw. Eventually, we will be playing until age group 80-Plus as the men already are. Now the Women's draw stops at 50-Plus.

"Sylvia. How old are you?" I ask.

"I'll be 37 soon."

"Uhm. How old do you think I am?"

Pause.

"I bet you don't think I'm almost 51."

"I knew you were OLD, but I didn't know how o—," she responds, even as I hit her playfully in the ribs with my racquet and exclaim, "Pooh!"

These Canadians have a nice mixture of expertise, seriousness of play, and courteous rivalry. The "clobber them at any cost" mentality of some Americans is absent. In Canada softball squash is considered a non-contact sport. It emphasizes good sportsmanship and includes grace and humor even in the midst of tight scores.

This Nanaimo Vets tournament is a barometer of where I am and what I need to do in order to secure my place in a higher level of play. It is also a chance to practice enjoying the social aspects of a tournament.

I have made a slight reputation from earlier tournaments and those wins can't be taken away from me. My move up a level is timely, even though I expect to get beaten often and I will not take home prizes. Losing and learning is worth it. Adding to the positive milieu of these Vets tournaments is worthwhile.

At Catherine Molnar's Carey House Bed 'n' Breakfast a hot water bottle is warming the sheets of my bed. Having seen a poster for a Women's tournament in Kamloops and hearing from some players that it is not to be missed, I ask Catherine if she knows any Quakers in Kamloops. Since Catherine has been on a committee with the only Quaker in Kamloops, she is able to give me his name and phone number. If I can get billeted, I will enter the Women's Weekend tournament in Kamloops. The dates coincide with my spring break and I have never been to interior British Columbia.

Preparing

I roll out of bed early, feeling stiff and groany, gulp a nutritious breakfast made in the blender, and get to the club early enough to do quiet stretching and warming-up on the treadmill and the Stairmaster.

My game is on. Denise is not very perky, but she tries. After losing, she says to Hilary, "Play *her* now, she's hot today." Then, looking back at me, Denise says, "I thought morning was not good for you."

I look down. "I know. I don't know what's wrong."

I play everyone there and blitz them. When they leave, I am still there, drilling or catching a game with a guy.

As Tamara leaves, she says, "Joy, you're obsessed. It's time to go home, do something else, greet the world."

"Well, I want to go to Worlds in 95, Masters Worlds. "

"Oh, are you really going? That's a year-and-a-half away."

"It's on my list."

"Ah, but then there are children—."

"That's right. I raised my kid, so now it's my turn."

We grin at each other and I comment, "Too bad we can't raise our kids from 40-60 and do our sports from 20 to 40."

"My sister did that. She's 40 and just had her first baby."

I nod and stretch out as part of my cool-down. My knees creak.

"Now if I can just remember the WD-40."

In the locker room, I notice two very tall women near the mirror, speaking a Scandinavian language. One is doing the other's hair and make-up. Both are in blue jeans and a tucked-in top. One is grand in stature and reminds me of Ayla in Jean Auel's novel *Clan of the Cave Bear*. As these women attend to each other, they burst into giggles. They seem very happy, very fresh, and very sensual. Their preoccupation with their sisterly beauty is strangely comforting to me. As I leave the locker room, however, I do not look at myself in the mirror.

Dreary Days

It is gray, windy and wet. From my bed I look out the window at the wet coldness. I want to stay in bed. But the voice and vision coming to me is clear. It is not mine; it is Nancy Kerrigan's. The skater is saying "GET UP" exactly the way she says it in her 30-second television spot after trying a jump and falling to the ice. So my motivated mind chants, "GET UP GET UP GET UP GET UP GET UP." And up I get.

Eventually, I put on running clothes and jog into the nearby park where no cars are allowed. It is my first outdoor running of the new spring. Starting with brisk walking and some stretching, I advance to jogging, running, and sprinting alternated with walking. This pattern I do three days in a row, and each time my sprinting becomes quicker.

Dreary Days

In the club's weight room I consult with the director of fitness. I have learned that at the training camp for the U. S. Women's Squash Team skill drills, strategy, and plyometrics are emphasized. Because jumping up or out is hard for me, the trainer takes me to the proper machine and adds two sets of plyometric pushes to my regular routine.

To keep my forearm strong for hitting overheads I need arm-strengthening exercises. The trainer starts me with a three-pound weight in both hands. I feel no resistance. She tries 5 pounds, 10 pounds, and finally 12 pounds. Looking surprised, the trainer says, "I want you to feel challenged."

On the court I practice a new-for-me service return, a three-wall from the backcourt, the Nancy Stern special.

At home while watching the 1994 Winter Olympics, I lie on my carpet and do crunches.

I read a basic squash book again—until I nod off to sleep. Vexed with myself, I ask, *"Is this dozing off an age-related reaction, a reaction to training, or both? How long will it take me to feel spry again?"*

When I feel brave, I check my torso for fat, my thighs for noticeable quadriceps and my hip joints for arthritic pain.

One morning my nerves get tested. A screeching noise from next door, a gardener's leaf sucker-upper, takes me by surprise. I stomp to my porch and scream at the worker to turn it off, it is "TOO LOUD!" Of course, he doesn't hear me. But I feel better. Coming inside and calming down, I ask myself why I have reacted in this way. *"That's something I would do if I had PMS."* Turns out I do. *"Oh, for Pete's sake, a period, maybe my last one ever. Should I celebrate or lament?"*

I flash back to age 14 when my strength and vitality were enormous. I did all the sports the boys did, often played with them, excelled at everything I tried, and was frisky as a colt. If I could combine that friskiness with the skill, cunning, and super-fitness I am achieving now in my fifties, I might have a better chance on the squash court. That's what I want and can't have—the advantages of both youth and age!

My accommodation to age is to make sure I do a thorough warm-up before even a casual match, so that I practice at my highest potential level and avoid injury.

A few days before time to leave for the next Vets tournament in Vancouver, Denise and I play. I am revved up; Denise is not. As we stretch together, Denise reveals what she is up to.

"I'm still working on my research. My mind's kinda there, not here. It's on what I'm doing. I get so absorbed."

"I was proud of us the other day." I put in. "On the Monday holiday when we came in to play, you had been doing research all day, I had been editing a dissertation written by a friend of mine, and Mary had been working on her master's thesis. We three had been thinking hard and then came here to play hard."

"Yeah, I'm feeling the pressure to publish now. I like what I am doing and am willing to put the time in."

"Denise, I have never put this spin on it before, but I don't think we'd find the same thing among the men squash players—at least in this club."

"You may be right. The guys here—they think work is something you do as a function. You do it and then come here. Don't carry it with you. They are so surprised that I work so hard, and they wonder about me when I say I can't play on weekends and holidays because I have to go into my office and work."

"Yes, you are motivated, Denise."

"Huh uh. They pay me well, but I work hard for it."

"And another thing, my house." Denise goes on. "A couple of the guys have come over to look at things, the plumbing and so forth. It's a really nice house. The way they look at me, I swear they're thinking, 'She's single, this isn't right. She's able to buy this new house herself. She's a woman, she's supposed to need a man's income to live in something like this.'"

""Oh well, let them think it. They'll get used to it. But they won't ever ask you out if they think you don't need them. Men like to feel needed, at least the older ones still do. Younger guys, I don't know what they're made of."

"Me neither. Anyway, that's another story. Let's hit some more."

We play and play. I turn it on. Denise is still a little spacey.

"You know, Denise, this is not a cut-throat duel. I'm going to try some new shots, but I'd like to win."

"Well, I should hope so." We laugh.

"Especially since I'm getting ready for a tournament and you're not, my ego is on the line, my reputation, not yours."

Skill and Cunning Vets Tournament
Evergreen Squash Club
North Vancouver, British Columbia, Canada

I get to the Evergreen Squash Club in Vancouver in plenty of time, missing a snowstorm by leaving directly from work at 3:00 p.m. Once here I have time to eat their traditional Friday night dinner of grilled sausage on a bun with sauerkraut and beer. There are six entries in Women's A, twelve in Women's B—130 entries total.

World Champion Joyce Maycock plays brilliantly again. In the change room I ask her how her match was. She says, "I almost beat a guy in the Men's 45 A Finals." When I ask her what she does to stay fit, she says, "Nothing extra. Just play a lot of squash."

"Do you do weights?"

"No strength training. Sometimes I run. I am not very good at running consistently and not very good at stretching either. I expect that as I grow older, it will catch up with me." After her shower she bolts out, first slipping her warm-up suit over her very trim body.

At the social time Joyce is talked about. One guy says, "She's bionic. She never tires." He has played her several times at these Vets tournaments and at first was quite conscious she was a woman, but after playing her a few times, his mind-set changed from "getting beat by a woman" to "getting beat by a very good player."

What are her secrets? What is her leg strength? Her forearm strength? What is her VO_2 score? Why is she fitter than the other Open level veteran women players? Is Joyce Maycock to squash what Janet Evans is to swimming?

My matches are not memorable. I play well but lose to younger players—Cathy Sullivan, Karen George, and Sylvia Strosel.

Because Evergreen doesn't have enough courts for the large draw, some of us play matches at the Hollyburn Country Club. Hollyburn has five international singles courts 21 feet wide, (one with a movable back wall to convert to a racquetball court length), one court 20 feet

Skill and Cunning Vets Tournament

wide with a movable back wall used mostly for racquetball, and one doubles court. For the experience of it, I hit on a doubles court and imagine the thrill of playing doubles or mixed doubles on it.

When I ask Sylvia for tips on improving my game, she tells me to hit the ball higher on the wall— to get it deeper. Hitting deeper gives you time to get back to the T.

Sylvia also advises that you must not be afraid to question an opponent's request for a let. If you wonder about the call, you should look at the referee in appeal. Eventually your looks will cause the ref to question her judgment and think maybe she's in error in awarding lets or strokes to your opponent. This is not bad sportsmanship, simply part of the psychological aspect of a match. Also, it is safer to call more lets.

The atmosphere at the dinner is relaxing and I get to see a new side of the squash bunch. For instance, during the raffle drawing, the fellow who wins the raffle stands up to secure his prize—a white terry-cloth robe. In order to get his prize he is supposed to disrobe the mannequin on which the robe has been draped. Catcalls and whistling pierce the room as he graciously walks behind the mannequin, strokes her quite subtly, and unties her belt. The disrobing reveals a bright red bra and black garter belt decorated with red ribbons. People giggle. I wonder if anyone is offended, but I don't say anything. "Offended" is the buzzword in the United States these days, what with political correctness and all.

During award presentations Dave Adams, the tournament director and emcee, stumbles over his tongue as he consistently refers to the players as "guys" and then adds the term "girls."

This faux pas reminds me of something I notice on the

club's bulletin board— about women, that is, older women who play squash. The entry form for an upcoming tournament north of Vancouver reads, "Men, Women and Vets." When I ask a man from the sponsoring club whether "Vets" means men or women, he tries to wiggle out of the oversight and concedes that it probably refers to men. So is it assumed that no older squash-playing women will enter this tournament? Where are the minds of the tournament directors?

Generally, Canadians take tournament customs with humor and good will, and the level of respect for women and for women who play is high. Something subtle is going on.

The Canadian women get around their status by organizing themselves very efficiently and promoting events such as Women's Weekends. On these weekends in Victoria and Kamloops, competitive play is for women only and men are discouraged from hanging around the courts.

As I leave Vancouver I thank Friends Tim Bartoo and Ruth Walmsley for putting me up. Ruth is preparing for her trial for doing civil disobedience on Vancouver Island. She and others were arrested for refusing to disperse during a Meeting for Worship on logging roads, in a protest effort to prevent trucks from taking old growth logs out of the forest. Going to Vancouver Friends Meeting with Tim and Ruth on Sunday reminds me of the source of my athletic endeavors.

At home again I contemplate. Wide courts—my bugaboo. My inexperience on wide courts is hindering me. Not knowing what to do with that extra foot on the 21-foot courts is bewildering me. At the B level I have time to control for the extra width, to adapt, to rely on reduced ball speed and my opponent's errors. At the A level I need a higher level of skill and spryness. The logical plan is to hie myself to the wide courts at the Seattle Club and the women down there, including my nemesis, Mariza.

Still curious about my heart palpitations, I stop by my club's sports medicine doctor. He says: "Heart palpitations during competition might have something to do with extra epinephrine being released into the body during exercise. You produce so much epinephrine that when you stop suddenly after a point, your body doesn't know what to do with the excess, and so the heart and other organs have to adjust. This adjustment to stress might produce an irregular heartbeat. It is nothing to worry about, but keep in touch with a doctor and walk around after a demanding point."

Tamara Trying

Tamara and I play again but first we talk, as usual. "Joy, I woke up this morning in a cold sweat, thinking, 'Maybe I'm too old to do this, won't ever happen.' "

"How old?"

"Forty-three. We're going to use fertility drugs soon. I wish we were a normal couple. We've been doing this for five months. I'd like to go on another five. But my husband, now he says his job is threatened and we have to budget better."

Another day we play again. "How are *you* this morning, Tamara?"

"Oh, fine, I guess. My period came last night. It's funny. I was so sure I was pregnant. I felt different. My period was late. I had an enormous appetite."

"Well, maybe there was conception and it wasn't a—and your body did its wisdom."

"Yeah, maybe. Oh, Joy, I'm so tired of this. It's so emotional. I just want it to be over, one way or the other. I've got to talk myself into accepting this, this loss. Believing that having just one child is OK."

"Tamara, the way I see it, you're not losing anything, you're just not gaining anything. It's important to keep the quality of what you have."

"That's really right, Joy. Well, a couple more months of this, we'll try a few more times, although it's expensive, this artificial insemination. All these hormones, this progesterone is making me sick, the side effects. They didn't tell me I'd get headaches. They see so many women; I think they forget it's new for each woman. I asked a whole lot of questions. I took it on faith that they knew what they were doing, what was going to happen to me, but these side effects."

"Well, as long as you feel passionate about it."

"Yes. Hey, let's play. I'm feeling so aggressive; I want to slug the ball across the entire club. You know, I've spent the last two weeks looking at my underpants!"

Ethereal Effects

This Quickie tournament features the regular assortment of fellows, plus Tamara, Denise, and me. On the bench we are resting, sweaty and pleasantly tired. We are within hearing distance of some guys.

Between big breaths, Tamara says to me, "You had some really good shots out there."

"Thanks," I say, "you played great, Tamara. Better than in practice."

"Yeah, fierce women," she says while looking at the fellow who is grinning at us. We return his grin.

"Your drop shots are so good, Joy. You have such poise."

"Well, thank you."

"What gives me the most pleasure is when someone thinks I'm gonna hit it in one corner, and I change at the last minute and put it in the other."

"You're deceitful, Tammy," says the guy.

"I love squash," continues Tamara. "Once I called up my mother and told her, 'I love squash. It's so deceitful.'" She said, 'That's nice dear.'"

I look carefully at Tamara. "We both come on as such goody-two-shoes. Basically, this game is cutthroat—."

"I know, but when I get on the court—it's like my evil twin comes out."

"Yup," I concur.

The guy tries to look sensitive, to understand.

"Joy, you're so much better now, and fitter," says Tamara. "When I first met you and played you, you were fatter and not toned. Your face got red. Now it's different. Now you've got control and poise. You wait for the right time. I wish I could remember to wait. I just rush it."

Coach walks by.

I say, "Thanks, Coach, for having the tournament!"

He smiles, "Uh, huh, you played great."

"Well, thanks," I mumble. "I wish these courts were wide courts. In Canada last week I had trouble adjusting to their wide courts. At the level I am playing, it matters."

"You can adjust. It doesn't take long. I play once a week on them."

"At the downtown club?"

"Yeah."

"Any chance of getting a wide court here?"

"Nah. I'd *like* to get a fourth court, in place of the child-

Court Quest

care area—"

I nod politely, while in my head the screaming starts: "No! Not after all these years of trying to get childcare in places like this!"

We resume watching a match. The thud of squash balls hitting walls and racquet strings is a comforting noise. The slightly sweaty smell wafting through the ventilation system is also comforting because it belongs here. Coach walks around, organizing players, chatting, doing what he is good at.

I sit on the bench daydreaming:

The women are ready to play. Joy wins the serve. They start at 0-2, Tamara at two points due to the handicap format.

Tamara grins. Joy grimaces. In a few minutes it is 5-0 Tamara. Joy adjusts. She begins running faster, gutting it out, grunting to get deep balls back deeply. Tamara has some unforced errors.

They are playing in a brilliant light. At this moment Tamara is "Madonna Momma" because the day before she was inseminated with her husband's sperm. She is on Clomid. Five eggs are ready. Now a shimmering light extends around her body, enveloping Joy, too. In slow motion they lunge and stretch and swing for everything, moving in hallowed perfection, exhibiting their Holy Prowess.

I come to and look around the courts. Then I daydream again:

Between points Joy is panting hard. She gets scared. A Voice Over overrides her panting: "OK, you know your heart's going to calm down, your breathing is going to slow down. Don't worry! You can recover! My God, don't forget your VO2 score broke the chart!" She remembers to breathe deeply at the beginning of each serve.

In the background she hears sounds of laughter and goodwill, of whooping and hollering. She wins the first game, 15-14, the second, 15-9.

Later as we women leave the courts for the locker room, we walk past a guy Tamara likes to hit with.

"So, how's your sperm count?" quips Tamara.

"Dangerously high," says the guy.

"And what about the motility?"

"Good."

Chuckles all around.

"And what about your volume?" says Tamara, looking insouciant.

"Volume? All it takes is one...."

"But tonight," says Denise, "she needs five—." Laughter and giggles regale from us as we walk into the locker room, arms around each other's shoulders in camaraderie.

"Well," says Denise, "I think they think we're hammered."

We wrap ourselves in towels and happy faces, long hair flowing down our muscular shoulders and backs. Gracefully we walk around the locker room, preparing to re-enter our other worlds. A flickering light makes our appearance heaven-like. At this time and in this light age doesn't matter much. We walk the walk of healthy women.

Women's Weekend Tournament
Racquetor Club
Kamloops, British Columbia, Canada

Nine international courts. One doubles court. Good viewing area. Glass back walls. Some bleachers. Lounge for dining and drinking. Pro shop.

The owner of the Racquetor, located across from the University College of the Cariboo, is John Sagan. At first John envisioned the building that had housed a racquetball club as a storage warehouse for videos, to supply his increasingly popular video stores. Fortunately for squash players, John was persuaded to convert the racquetball courts to squash courts and to upgrade the club. The Racquetor has become one of the best places for large tournaments in Western Canada and was the home of Canadian Nationals in 1993.

Women's Weekend 1994 has only forty-eight entries, somewhat low due to injuries and the date coinciding with family spring vacations. The theme this year is "The Fifties." Costumes are almost mandatory.

After I arrive at the Racquetor and change into playing clothes, I go onto a court to hit. Then I hang out to chatter a bit. One of the organizers comes up to me and introduces herself: "And you're Joy? I'm Debbie."

We shake hands.

"And you're how old?"

"51 in a few days."

I hear another woman say, "That's Joy from Seattle, and she's 50."

"You look great," says Debbie.

"Thanks."

"I must say, squash is a good—."

"Oxygenizer?"

"Good for fitness. I've never seen anyone so fit-looking at 50."

I have observed ordinary folks in a Kamloops supermarket and conclude that Kamloops is a very dry place. Skin dries out earlier here than in rainy places like Seattle. People look dried out before their time. To me women in their forties look like they are in their fifties.

Before my first match Wendy MacDonald asks me who I am playing. I tell her Cathy Sullivan. We agree the courts are hot. I ask Wendy what to do, therefore. She says, "Well, you know what to do." I say, "I forget, tell me again." Right then she doesn't answer, but begins to introduce me to some women in the locker room by saying I am the one with the great *lob*.

I remember this advice and lobbing becomes part of my game plan, that is, play my own game, play it classic, and remember to lob.

Cathy is an experienced player. I lob a lot and win the first game. After losing the second and third games using my standard hard serve, I change to a lob serve and win the fourth game.

I feel strong and fast enough on the hot courts. My focus lapses one or two times and both times I lose the point. At the end of the fourth game I am out of breath, but I self-talk my heart rate down while sitting with closed eyes. My heart rhythm becomes slower and my breathing calms down. Recovery between points and games is excellent—thanks to my trainer and the beloved Stairmaster.

In the fifth game I go back to my hard serve, mainly

from the left, thinking she might be a little tired and a little off and knowing that I get stronger well into a match. I adjust my return of serve because her overhead serve is coming in a little low to be taken on the volley. I change to a backhand defensive lob. I miss a couple of serves to my forehand because I am standing too close to the wall, not turned sideways enough. A couple of times I hit a deep backhand off my right leg rather than my left, but I gut out enough lift. Even though I tin a couple of forehand two-wall returns, I try again and get her several times. I get a run of points. I am up 8-4 or so and then it goes to 8-8.

We go handout once and Cathy tins. I take a deep breath, and serving from the right, hit an overhead serve as hard and as high as I can. The ball hits the back wall low and bounces out far. Cathy lunges and tins it. Match over. I win, 3-2. Game scores are 10-9, 4-9, 3-9, 9-7, 10-8.

Later Cathy says her wrist is bothering her because of too much feeding balls to the junior players she has been coaching.

At the last Vets tournament Cathy beat me, so this is a good win for me. Not expecting to go five games with her, I thought if I got one game and looked like a true A level player, I would be pleased.

After walking off the court, I don't acknowledge the onlookers, since I am not acquainted with anybody who is watching. A couple of the Kamloops women, noticeable by their outlandish 1950's garments, say, "Good match, hard match, well fought match." I shake my head, "I can't figure how it went my way." Then staring at one woman's blue felt full-circled skirt with a white poodle cutout on its front, I say, "It must have been the 50's influence! I was in my prime in the 50's."

Women's Weekend Tournament

My advantage is a day of rest, having arrived a day before the tournament started. Cathy spent four hours today in a car driving from Vancouver to Kamloops.

Between matches I learn about a rare disorder associated with exercise. Some athletes sometimes go into anaphylactic shock if they exercise. A few hours before playing, they have to take antihistamine. If they are caught in a reactive episode after a game, they must give themselves adrenaline to counter their body's extreme reaction to whatever chemicals are released 20-30 minutes into vigorous exercise. For this disorder athletes may end up in a hospital emergency room. I count my blessings.

In another match I play Sandy Glass, age 28. Strong, blonde, and sturdy, she is a very hard hitter with no weakness as far as I can tell. Quickly it goes 3-0 Sandy. I get two points. The third game and the last half of the second, I get some winners for handouts, mostly by doing drop shots. Sandy is an all-around talented player on her way to the Open Division. I think, *"If I had started earlier and played in college, I would have been able to play like you, Sandy."*

Bonnie Price from Kamloops is another player in the Round Robin. After losing a four game match with lots of lets to Cathy Sullivan, Bonnie is tired. My game is on. I have good backhand returns from deep, repetitive rails. Only one stroke goes against me— from a caroming ball— and no lets.

Referee Nancy Stern calls a foot fault on me from the left box. Later she explains that I am sliding my left foot across the red line of the service box before hitting the ball, mostly on lob serves. This gives me unfair advantage because from this position I am able to get to the T more quickly.

I outplay Bonnie and would have, I believe, even if she had been fresher.

Saturday night at the Racquetor is hilarious. To start things off a local group of men and boys sing tame and sweet songs from the Fifties. Then they leave and the women do the entertaining—risqué jokes, take-offs, songs, and an impersonation of Elvis Presley. Almost provoking a riot of hollering is the "Mr. Sandman" song sung by the women from Prince George and featuring photos of well-built men taped to squash racquets. To everyone's delight the women bounce around flashing their flashlights at each refrain, singing, "Bumbumbumbumbumbumbumba, bum-bumbumbumboom, Mr. Sandman."

It is PJs night and there is a prize for the best PJ costume. Before the dinner, there is a fashion show by local players dressed up as 50's girls, with a narrative take-off on odd items like mules, those open heel and open toe slippers of the old days. An abundant dinner features dessert—huge make-it-yourself-banana-splits-with-all-the-toppings-you-ever-asked-for-as-a kid-and-didn't-get.

Oodles of door prizes, enough for every entrant, entice us. Prizes include T-shirts, writing paper, address books, diaries, and wine. My door prize is a light blue diary.

After dinner the women play games. Who among us can fold a paper airplane and throw it down from the viewing area above a squash court into a cardboard box resting on the T? After an hour and hundreds of paper planes, someone finally lands her airplane in the box for a nice prize— a heavy shirt-jacket. Who can putt golf balls through long cardboard map-holder tubes into a basket? Who can stroke a ball into an upside down football helmet? Who can push a ball onto a mini-rubber mattress? (We can try as many times as we wish, then record our score on a piece of paper.) Who can blow the biggest bubble from pink bubble gum? Who can hula the hula hoop the longest and the goofiest? Some women lie down and twirl the hoop around their upstretched legs. Zany laughter and giggles. Whooping and hollering. High spirits abounding.

I am curious about the women themselves—which ones love women rather than men, and do the former feel unable to participate in the entertainment of poking fun at the traditional roles of men and women? Do the women who prefer women feel out of it and unappreciated? Surely the British Columbia women aren't unaware. Perhaps they think it is not necessary to show inclusiveness, as people are feeling obligated to do in the USA. On the other hand, maybe the Canadians are way ahead of the Americans on this issue.

Most of the women here are shirts-out types. Only a few are dressing as though men were around. One woman says, "Oh, it's no matter how you look, you're in Kamloops." Some players make a point of mentioning husband and children as they exclaim about how great it is to get away for the weekend.

I linger next to the respected Claire Johnson, a long-time organizer of squash in Kamloops.

"So, Claire, you're not playing?"

"No, bad vertebra and arthritis in my ankles and feet."

"Oh, sorry about that. Might you play again later?"

"Maybe, after surgery. I'm trying to avoid that, but how long on pain can one live? I don't know."

"When you were playing, what level did you play?"

"Oh, A. But I promised my husband I wouldn't get competitive. I had taken some time off, and when I went back, I said I wouldn't get competitive, would play only for recreation."

"You mean you would have been in the Open Division?"
"Yes, I think so. But I would've had to train, and my—."
"Oh."

Dismayed, I feel sorry for her. Is she another female player of potential excellence deterred by a preference for domestic peace? That is, held back by her husband?

At midnight Saturday I arrive at my host's home. The house is quiet. The moon is bright and full. There are no streetlights. I feel an eagerness to talk to my host. He would say, "How're you?" and then I'd talk about the tournament. But who greets me is not the man; it's the exquisite golden retriever who lives there. The oldest child, a boy, is asleep in the living room with a bunch of friends—a sleepover birthday party. The middle girl is in her bedroom recovering from staying overnight with a girlfriend, and the little girl is in her bedroom. My host is asleep, recovering from organizing the birthday party, shopping and cooking, and taking his college students on a field trip early this morning. Tomorrow the family drives south to Vernon, B.C. and takes part in Friends Meeting for Worship.

On Sunday I play Gina Hohenwarter from Vancouver's Evergreen Club. Gina is 37, a former ballroom dancer, and looks stunning in a black leotard and a black pleated skirt. I am comfortable in an oversized white squash T-shirt and my forever-hot pink Lycra tights.

Gina handles my serves, lobs, and mid-court volleys well. She is very quick. In the second game I change from a hard serve to a lob serve or side serve and then drop her return for a winner. I win this game and the next one. During the 90-second break before the final game Gina goes upstairs to talk to her club friends, "What should I do? What should I do?"

"Boast," is the answer. So she does, from mid and backcourt. I am caught flat-footed. More often than not, Gina puts away my scrambling defensive return of boast. Sometimes my return comes straight out at me for a let or a stroke to Gina. We play to 5-5 in the fifth. At 6-5 Gina, I think, *"That's it, I don't know what to do."* Gina beats me in five games to win the Women's A Consolations. Our scores are 9-5, 1-9, 2-9, 9-5, 9-5.

Later I see a woman making a chart of Wendy MacDonald's match with Nancy Stern and learn that she is marking where the ball is played for a point or a handout and what type of hit it is, for instance, a crosscourt, rail, or boast. She is trying to find patterns of play.

After my final match I play a couple of friendly games with Shannon McJannet. Shannon has been very friendly, and asked me to sit at her table for the Saturday night fest. She says, "I wish you played at my club in Vancouver." Driving out of Kamloops together we caravan south over the Coquihalla Highway towards Vancouver. Later Shannon calls me in Seattle to make sure I have arrived home safely.

Loss, Infatuation, and Decision

In Seattle at a Quickie Tournament Tamara is sitting with her son on the floor. Both are looking beautiful. From a distance I mouth the words, "How are you? How are you feeling?"

Tamara's lips move quietly, " I lost it."

"Oh."

"Yes," looking at her son, she signals me to be circumspect.

I read her lips: "Well, I haven't lost it yet, but I will, next week."

My face registers questions. Tamara whispers, "There's something wrong with it. It's not growing right. The hormone count isn't going up as fast as it should. The beta-HCG level is supposed to increase faster than it has the first few weeks."

I gaze at her empathically. "So it's still in there? An embryo? Just one?"

"Yes, one. It's early yet. Six weeks."

"The pregnancy test still shows positive? It's not a false positive?"

"No. And I've got other symptoms. I'm really sore through here," grazing her breast area with a hand.

"What a weird state to be in."

"I know. It is. But you know, the one good thing that's come from all of this? Weight training. I started one of the weight and strength training classes and I love it. I'm going to stick with it. I feel strong and full."

"Cool. Talk to you later."

I recede towards a squash court as Tamara gives my racquet-free hand an affectionate squeeze. I am thinking, *"Oh dear, another try at her age. Why are they doing this?"*

A woman is playing a guy. They are moving well and making some good shots. The woman is being outplayed but is going down valiantly. Onlookers let out a loud "whoop and holler" from the viewing area whenever there is an extra good rally or a lucky shot.

On a bench near the courts waiting to play, Denise is watching this match. Brendan is a tall, Gaelic-looking, graceful guy, a real hunk.

"Who's that?" I ask.

"That's Brendan. He's just back after being gone for some time, to Belize. He's single and incredibly good-looking."

Loss, Infatuation and Decision

"Do you know him very well yet?"

"Not yet. I asked somebody who he is and she told me and said she can't remember what he does for a living, and I said, 'I don't care! Just let me look at him.'"

"Yeah. I took a good look at him, then I looked at you, and my mind, it put you together."

"Really, " says Denise as Tamara walks up to our bench.

"Uh, I told Tamara, I'm in love. No. I'm in lust! It's been too long."

We giggle.

"You know," says Denise, "I have this friend, and she's getting married soon. She's my age. She wants children, too. She's got her career all set and everything. Well, she met this guy and she says she knew the first night that he was the one."

"You mean love at first sight," says Tamara.

"Yes. I don't understand that. I mean, you think you've got it all figured out, what you want in a man. But I can't get past my list: "Good sense of humor, athletic—"

"Uh huh. It's hard to find someone both athletic and academic, like you," I chime in.

"Right. The men at the university, they're too—"

"Scroungie," I conclude.

"Yes. Besides, they're mostly all married."

"Uh huh."

"But this love at first sight thing. I wonder about it. My friend and her intended, by the time they get married, they will have known each other for only a year. But she's convinced." For a moment Denise looks solemn and lost in thought.

Through more laughter I remind myself: *"For me it was love at first sight. He does have both the athletic and the academic."*

Mr. Hunk plays several guys gallantly and skillfully.

121

Finally in the Finals he loses by a couple of points. He takes the loss like a gentleman.

The Vetter the Better Tournament
Hollyburn Country Club
West Vancouver, British Columbia, Canada

The Hollyburn tournament is the last Masters circuit tournament of the 1993-94 season. I have entered with high hopes. If I compete again in the summer it will most likely be against women of younger ages, almost always a daunting experience.

For this tournament my warm-up is stretching, plus 10 minutes on the treadmill at Pace 3.1 and Gradient 4, plus huge lunge-walking in the gym and some fancy foot practice.

My equipment checks out OK—HiTec shoes with Thorlo socks, white shorts and a baggy shirt. I tuck my braid into my headband so it can't flop around and distract me between points.

My foresight is right-on about attire. This tournament is "All Whites, Will Be Enforced." I have brought a new outfit with me. When I found at Nordstrom Seattle a skirt with a pastel border on the bottom and a pretty matching top decorated with embroidered racquets that could be squash racquets, I couldn't resist the outfit.

Both Sylvia Slosel and Wendy MacDonald want something special for their matches, too. When I overhear Sylvia and Wendy talking about getting new outfits at Hollyburn's Pro Shop, I show them mine. Graciously, Sylvia declines to buy the one featured on the mannequin because it looks too much like my new outfit. We laugh about this coincidence, joking how it would be if we all showed up in the same outfit. When Wendy says we should get our pictures taken together, I take her up on it. Sylvia's boyfriend takes the picture with my camera. We look like high school cheerleaders.

In my match against Hilda Ward, I play well— turning, moving out of the way, circling, watching, getting balls, staying calm, calling lets and getting some strokes! My goals are three:

To not give away the first four points.

To not get strokes against me.

To move my feet faster and take smaller steps.

In the first game I am up three points to none with no unforced errors and no lets or strokes against me. This spoils my pattern of botching the first four points before settling down. But I lose in extra points 10-8. The second game goes by quickly. I lose in a blitz 9-2. In the third game I am ahead by four when Hilda turns on the steam and for no good reason I decide to change my serve, losing 10-9.

Tall and slim, Hilda is a smart player and when she needs to, she can change tactics. When I change to hitting short in an effort not to hit to her mid-court forehand—her "stun drive," she dribbles in shots for winners and creams me with backhand boasts from mid-court.

People are watching, focused. Later Shannon congratulates me for going to points against Ward, "a premiere player." At 45, she is still very fast and runs to everything. Sometimes she errs— hits it out or tins when she rushes and scrambles, doesn't set up well enough.

My serves are good; none are out. I take time to set up and breathe deeply before each serve. I focus on a charcoal smudge high on the front wall. But my service returns from my backhand are not good enough— too often a crosscourt, rarely a rail, sometimes a good drop. In the third game I do better on returning rails.

I get taught a lesson, though! Sometimes when Hilda is serving, she starts the next serve before I am ready. Frequently, the referee says the new score immediately after the point stops, and quickly Hilda walks into the opposite service box and serves, often without looking at me to see if I am ready. As a consequence my returns are sloppy. Later Shannon tells me that sometimes at the serve I look as if I am not ready. In this case I could let the ball go by me for an automatic let, telling the referee I am not ready.

Upon asking Wendy about continuous play, I learn there is no set time between points. "The rule is a reasonable amount of time," she explains. So, don't step into the service box until you're ready to receive the serve. If your opponent serves when you are not in the box, it's a let. If that strategy doesn't work, between games, say to the referee that the other player is serving before you are ready. The referee then might adjust the pace by delaying saying the score and reminding the server to wait until her opponent is ready.

Wendy's husband compliments me. "You have a graceful way, you look certain you know exactly where the ball is going." In truth, I now "see" the point dynamics with a more mature vision. No more am I a scrambling neophyte.

The ratio has changed—from 70% pluckiness and 30% skill to something closer to 50-50. I don't hit myself with the ball or with the racquet. I call let on a "round." I don't collide with anybody. I am hitting harder and running well. I am more accustomed to the wide court. Of course, I still

The Vetter the Better Tournament

need practice hitting for length, positioning, and selecting shots. Indeed, my level has gone up another notch.

The next day I am scheduled to play two matches. First, I ref an easy match of D level men. Then I am paired with a relatively weak player. Our match tests me. I win 3-0 in controlled play with a "deep to drop" strategy. I cut off my opponent's serves and go for winners. The win is fairly easy, but I could have erred out. I drop the first three points of the first game and get one stroke against me, but after that I settle in.

My match with Sylvia is quick. It is the third time in a row we have played each other in the Consolation Finals. Each time she prevails. This match is 3-0 Sylvia with only a few points to me. Sylvia plays snappily and hits well. I get stuck behind her on two-wall shots and misread her rails. Rather than anticipating a deep rail and staying on one side, I go to the T and can't move back in time.

After our three official games we play a friendly game where I hit lob serves and do better. Sylvia lets me win 9-5 and wonders why I don't hit more lob serves.

About the age thing: Sylvia says she is 37 and feeling old. "If I play half as well as you at 51, I'll be happy."

"Well, you can get better. I've gotten a lot better in a year. If you improve every year, you'll be REALLY good in 15 years!"

We have a good laugh envisioning this ludicrous notion.

At the dinner dance I make a fun time of it. I am invited to sit at a table with Mona and Don Gunn from Squamish. Don buys me a glass of wine and our table shares two bottles of wine. We chatter about squash.

The dancing starts after the roast beef dinner. At first I stand aside, then decide it is too great a night to be a no-fun kid. Mona decides the same, so we dance a four-some with two guys. This group dancing starts my "heck-with-it" attitude, so eventually I walk over to some fellows I know to nod to. I ask, "Which one of you wants to dance?" and since one of them does, we dance. Then Sylvia picks up on the scene and invites me to dance with her and her boyfriend. Later I join their table. Almost often enough I am asked to dance or I do the asking. My energy is enormous. When an image of dancing with my beloved back in Seattle pops into my mind, I squash it.

Door prizes given randomly to dancers mean I get a prize—massage sessions from Sylvia for back pain! We laugh. With this much playing and dancing, no way will I need therapy for back pain! I give the certificate to a guy at our table who plays and is fine but whose wife is not present due to chronic back pain.

I look presentable in black slacks, a pink pearl sweater, a pearl necklace and earrings. My hair is up. I feel grateful for a luxurious evening in a first class place with healthy people.

Deciding for Lessons

The next week in Seattle I play Leslie Seman. We play aggressively. I turn it on and win. I am a little nervous but determined because I can't bear to lose to a woman from my club.

After the match Coach gives me a wide smile. Suddenly I announce, "I want a lesson."

My Vision-Over shows lots of lessons and dollars floating above the court. But no matter, I learn quickly. I express a decision to go forward, to get better, so I will deserve to go to United

States Nationals, even though I might go broke getting there.

My decision to start lessons is in spite of, not because of, anything in my personal life to support it. Rob continues to withdraw, is not around much. He is deeply upset. Officially informed that he will have to retire at the end of this academic year, for reasons of age and medical impairment, he is trying to adjust to a new future. I am upset too, and stubbornly we try to function as usual. We won't let ourselves be frozen by the inevitable changes we foresee. Rob's approach to our inevitable parting is to diminish slowly, gradually over time. My preference is to keep on as intensely as ever and then have a dramatic, heart-felt, tearful wrenching apart. Rob's approach will prevail.

My quandary continues. It is not simply love him or leave him. It is more like love him, not leave him, and lose him anyway. He will relocate. He will be rejoining his wife who will look after him. Having no weight in this decision, I try, as always, for control and compassion, controlled compassion. Loving each other from afar is a poor option.

One day while walking alone, I find a penny gleaming in the spring sun. Great joy from such a small sign fills my heart.

Playing is uppermost in my mind, at least my surface mind. As usual I am functioning on two levels at least—the daily level of work and play as well as the subterranean level of my long relationship with Rob.

"Old Man River, that Old Man River, you just keep rolling, you just keep rolling, you just keep rolling along." That song speaks to us.

Recent weeks of hitting with men have got me focused on running and pacing. With women I focus on shot skills and court movement. Often we play the "Long Game," a method of hitting to length.

At the daily level I am remiss, avoiding the weight room, so I meet with my trainer to get back on the training track.

The trainer counsels, "This is a good amount of weight and reps for you."

"Yup. Feels fine so far," I grunt as I complete a leg press.

"Uh, I'd like to know what it would take to blow you out of the water."

We move on to a wrist-strengthening weight and bench exercise. Trainer kneels on the bench with one knee, balances herself with one hand, and holds a 10-pound barbell in the other hand. She bends her open wrist downward and upward.

"So, this is how you do it, slowly, completely, feeling the muscles in your forearm. Now you try it."

I try it with a 12-pound barbell.

"You'll want to do four sets of this and then ask, to get a better reading, if this is a good amount of weight and reps for you for this exercise."

"OK, feels fine at this."

"Go for it."

On other days I get instruction and attention from other trainers. I complain about various minor aches and pains in my muscles. I am introduced again to the plyometrics machine, to train my legs to push off explosively—like high caliber skiers using their legs beautifully.

When I stay away from the courts for more than a few days, my doubts take over Sometimes I stay home and only imagine I am in the weight room. Sometimes my body talks back by showing arthritic stiffness. Getting off a couch is painful. I walk stiffly and slightly bent over. I feel my age.

One Saturday a few of the women from the Seattle Club

play with us in a Round Robin. Mariza and I hit. We are pleasant with each other. Mariza plays well. I do not.

I am learning to play with newly changed contact lenses. They have been fashioned so that one eye focuses on far away things and the other eye focuses on mid-length things. For things really close up I have to use cheater glasses. On the court I can't wear cheaters because they don't come in eye guard versions. At first, watching the squash ball as it moves towards me and away again feels strange. While hitting with Mariza, my balance is off. I don't play well but have an excellent excuse.

I try out a joke about using a contact lens version of granny glasses, but it falls flat. The other women aren't into bifocals yet.

Ranking In British Columbia

After we finish our games, Mariza starts talking about tournaments.

"Joy, you've been going to the Canadian tournaments. I want to do those next year. They have ranking. You're ranked, you know. I read it on a memo they sent to us at my club. You're number one in the 50-55 age group."

"Really? I didn't know. It must be based on the number of points I got just for playing the Masters Tournaments."

"No, it's a real ranking by the British Columbia Squash Association. I'll show you sometime. You went to the Women's tournament? In Kamloops? You should have called me. I wanted to go, but I didn't want to drive by myself. Was it good, did you think it was worth it?"

"Yes, great, really great." Suddenly I shield myself. I nod and don't volunteer anything.

My ranking at the end of the 1993-94 squash racquets

season, based on the results of all the British Columbia tournaments in which I competed, is:

    Women Age 50-55 # 1
    Women Age 45-50 # 7
    Women Age 40-45 # 9

Seattle City Championships

 A few days later I am sitting near the courts, reflecting on playing tips. Coach's comments are flooding my brain: *"Watch the ball. Watch the bounce. Bend. Wait. Racquet up. Back to the T."*

 Denise corrals me.

 "So, are you going to enter the City Tournament?"

 "I haven't decided yet. I'm being ambivalent." My eyes cast down.

 "Well, I am, and Leslie is."

 "When is the deadline?"

 "Soon. Let's find out."

 We look at a posted entry form.

 "It's one day *before* this day. Well, I guess that settles that!"

 Denise looks relieved.

 "I could call. They don't do the draw right away," I toy.

 "Yes, call Sue Lehr. She'll let you in, especially if they need someone to fill a spot in the draw."

 "I'll give it serious consideration."

 From the observation bleachers above the courts I watch Denise and Leslie play their matches. Leslie comes from behind to beat Mariza when she tires. Leslie plays her best ever. Off court she beams triumphantly from this win.

 Denise wins the Women's B Final rather easily.

My Voice-Over chastises: *"I could be down there on that court. Would I have played Mariza, Leslie, or Denise? It is a small draw. The really good women played in the Men's draw or didn't enter. Except for chicken me. I didn't want to get beat in public by anybody I should be able to beat. I want to get better before I compete again. I am taking lessons. I am in the midst of a personal crisis. My focus is elsewhere, not on competing. I'm not willing to work out and diet in order to be in top form for competition. It's not wise to compete half-heartedly. I'm feeling blue."*

I leave the court for home, my mind on Rob and the situation. His heart condition has changed him, his life, and our lives. His last month of teaching— doing what he loves so much— is upon us. Soon he will be gone.

Now What?

The regular 1993-94 squash season ends. A few summer tournaments are scheduled, but mostly, people are doing outdoor things. My training momentum is slipping away.

Not looking forward to a tournament and doing the planning for it requires an adjustment. Will I continue my healthy eating, my exercise and training plan, my motivation? These are the main matters under my personal management. In other matters I have little or no voice. Someone else or an institution powers them.

I am a year older, a better squash player, and probably fitter than the year before, although maybe about the same fitness, adjusted for age. This is it. No glory. No title. No prize money. No clear plan for going ahead. I have high rankings in British Columbia age-group squash and of that

I am proud. But I am not registered for another tournament. Will I falter now?

I recall the intangibles of training and competing hard: the pure pleasure of playing, the excitement of the all-around uplift, and the outstanding physical health. These rewards distract me from wallowing in the pain of Rob's forced departure.

Meanwhile the outdoors beckons. As part of a new discipline I go running. I expect to feel slow and sluggish, cranking it out. But lo! I warm to it and sprint over the nearby wilderness park road—briskly, friskily. I feel I can run a long, long time and am amazed at how long I can maintain maximum sprint speed. I thought that after my brief dip into goal-free days and no squash, I would belong in the "Fit 50-Plus" program at the club. Yet my running shows me I am in fine condition. What is going on?

Is menopausal zest starting to rise? It has been a while since I have had a real period. At the onset of my last one in the spring, I predicted it might be my last. Oh well. I love having 14-year-old energy. I feel extremely grateful that I am healthy. Most of my friends have something seriously wrong with them or are held back by some physical factor such as poor coordination or bad eyes. Do I really stand out among my peers? How do I know? Does it matter?

Is going to United States Nationals in September in the cards for me?

Taking Action

Some things fall into place while others unbalance me.

A letter arrives from Squash B.C. It shows my ranking and congratulates me. I mention it to Rob and he says, "Attaway, kid, way to go." But we don't dwell on it. The bigger picture is on our minds, how our lives are changing. We dwell on the moments we still have for each other—and savor them.

Always adaptable, the next day I show the letter to Coach and ask him to help me get to U. S. Nationals, to help me train hard for it. He agrees. "I might go myself," he says.

I change to Ryka shoes. Ladies cut. They are for cross-training, but they work well on the court with Thorlo socks. Finally I have found a pair of athletic shoes narrow enough for my size 11AA foot. Wearing men's clodhoppers gets embarrassing. Stumbling over my own feet in way too-wide men's squash shoes is not pleasant.

My lessons continue. I become more graceful, fluid, skillful, and less winded. Occasionally Coach puts me in my place:

"You can't move around when your opponent is beginning to strike the ball."

"You mean I was moving backwards when you hit it."

"Yes. You can't do that."

(Giggling) "Actually, I can do anything I want to."

"No."

"It's not against the rules, is it?"

"No, but it's against the rules of winning squash."

"OK."

The entry form for U. S. Nationals in Baltimore, Maryland, appears in the summer issue of the USSRA NEWS. The dates are September 21-25, 1994, <u>before</u> fall quarter begins!

In my eagerness I fill out the application the very day it

Court Quest

arrives and mail it the next. The entry fee is $100 plus twenty dollars for an extra event. My main event is Women's 50-55. My extra event will be Women's B, if the Draw Directors find it wise. The decision depends partly on whether my age group plays a Round Robin or not. If it doesn't, I might play Women's B in addition to Women's 50-55. Playing in another age group is not permitted.

I make arrangements. Call my travel agent and get a reduced fare ticket. Get agreement from my department chairman to miss a faculty meeting the week before fall quarter begins. Write a postcard to the tournament's draw committee, asking if they know of a woman to share a hotel room with. Get a call from USSRA President Craig Brand with the name and number of Maggie McQuown in Irving, Texas. Call her. Fine. We will be at her hotel, the Radisson, where committee meetings will be held. (Maggie is an officer on the USSRA Board and sounds friendly and interesting.) All set.

Then it strikes me. Money is needed to finance this next level of questing. How will my days in Baltimore be paid for? The dreadful truth is that my quarterly contract for teaching at the college means I won't get paid until the end of October. September is always a lean month. Even though this quest means a lot to me, it doesn't mean so much that I am willing to break into my long-term investments. There must be some other way.

One option is refinancing my mortgage. I have been thinking about re-financing, and now my credit union is promoting a good rate. I can change from a variable rate of around 8% with my bank to a fixed rate of 7.5% with my credit union. So I refinance, adding to my current debt and promising myself that the lid is on.

Something gets in my way, however. I am training hard, taking lessons, doing weights, watching what I eat, and then whacko. While playing doubles ping-pong at a squash club barbecue, I get hit in the mouth by a ping-pong paddle. I am standing behind Penelope when she slams the ball. Her follow-through catches me on my mouth. The blow knocks me backwards onto the grass. One front tooth is fractured, the other damaged. Both teeth tilt inwards. Strangely I feel no pain.

I drive myself to the University of Washington Emergency Dental Clinic. The fractured part of the badly damaged tooth is removed and a root canal is started. Still there is no pain, no swelling, and no cut. I feel profoundly grateful that the damage is not greater.

This accident makes me hyper aware of my positioning on a court. The next time I play, as I look back at my opponent, I shield my face with my racquet and prepare to twist out of the way. As usual, I wear eye guards.

To what extent does my failure to sense danger reflect an attempt to have a grand time at that picnic regardless of my underlying angst? In what way was I not centered, and thus, not able to foresee such an event? Had I been listening to my Inner Light and realizing I was forcing gaiety, would I have avoided the ping-pong game? Was I failing to respect my dis-ease? Was I ignoring my decades of training as a practicing Quaker?

What other obstacles are looming? How prepared am I to refuse obstacles? It is past time to go to a Meeting for Worship and heed The Light.

More Hurdles

On this very beautiful Sunday morning I could be at North Pacific Yearly Meeting in Corvallis, Oregon. I could be hiking in the Cascades. I could be doing homework for my continuing education class.

I have decided to upgrade my qualifications for teaching English-as-a-Second-Language. An advanced certificate in teaching ESL could be a stepping-stone towards a better position at some other school.

On this very beautiful day no culturally induced distractions compel my notice. No dependent child, no expectant student, no lover— nobody generates the attitude that implies "Put me first, put yourself and your goals second." Therefore, I have no excuse for not accomplishing something important this day. No excuse!

I have to watch out for inertia as well as anxiety. Taking this grammar class is stressful. It is my first formal studying in over 25 years. I have chosen pass/no pass over a letter grade. Of the 13 classmates I have the most experience with the subject. What is telling to me personally is my reaction to the demands: I rev up unnecessarily and study too long. My fear of not meeting my high standards gets in the way of my efforts to pace myself graciously.

Again, I doubt what I perceive. Have I forgotten how competitive I am, even off the court? Is taking this course necessary? Will it interfere with my athletic goals? Can I do everything at once—study, teach, and train? Can I also complete the research project for which I have been awarded a faculty grant? Have I discerned The Light for this particular setting?

Even though discernment eludes me, I resume my training in earnest. Not sensing a nudge away from my

More Hurdles

ambitions, I conclude that I should center again on my goals. I enlist the help of my trainer and schedule myself into aerobics classes and weight training. The weather is hot and people prefer to do things outdoors, so there are fewer pick-up games at the club. I arrange for a lesson a week.

Life is getting expensive. I see myself as an athlete-in-training who needs a sponsor. I wish for funds to help me go to Nationals. Getting folks to contribute to the Women's National Squash Team is touchy, so a contribution for an ordinary competitor like me is out of the question. The sport of squash racquets is behind where it should be. In 1994 squash is not yet an Olympic sport. The participation and value of female competitors is especially underdeveloped.

Perhaps I am faltering through arrogance or *hubris* to believe that I am worth putting money, training, and effort into. But regardless of my age, my doubts, and my culture, my level of play begins to improve. Of course, I complain to Coach.

"It's a hurdle just being female in this twisty turny game. It doesn't help that I'm older, a little fat, and relatively unfit."

Coach counters with, "I'm old, fat, out of shape, and not as quick as I once was, but all that doesn't matter. If my shot is good enough, my opponent's return shot will not get me into trouble and I'll have time to get to the T."

Coach is good at coaxing me along. As I run hard to get back the balls he is giving me, he makes me run front to back, back to front and all the diagonals. He says, "Good hustle, stay with it, stay with it, that's it, stay with it." I need the encouragement.

Court Quest

One sunny morning at our Round Robin Hilary, Tamara, Leslie, Denise, and I are braving the indoor heat. We fiddle with our headbands and eye guards and adjust our skirts.

Denise says tactfully, "So, Joy, we did our birthday thing on Monday, sorry you had to work. I just had to go ahead and decide on a date. So we had a toast to you!"

"You did? That's nice."

"Yes," echoes Leslie, "A toast."

"Yes, to you, Joy," repeats Tamara.

I am pleased with the attention.

As usual, Tamara provides human-interest information. "So-and-so's former second wife just had a baby, because she's 41. No father, but she's very happy. I went to a shower for her, and I imagine she and her parents are just so happy that she's not married to so-and-so anymore, and you know his first wife after seven years of marriage decided she was a lesbian and left him for a woman friend."

"So, at the birthday thing you gossiped and had a grand time," I say.

"Well, yes, we goss—we talked about life events, what matters in life," Tamara says.

"Yes," says Denise. "We talked about life—philosophy of life, heavy stuff. By the time we left that restaurant, they were happy to see us go."

"Denise, now you can go to Nationals and play in 35-Plus and maybe win it!"

"Yeah, well—" she hedges.

"All these youngsters catching up with us makes me feel good," pipes in Leslie.

"Makes me feel good I can run with them spring chickens," chortles Tamara.

"So Denise, pretty soon you'll be seeing the effects of

More Hurdles

getting older." Tamara clutches her midriff. "My nutritionist said that it is perfectly natural to get heavier as you get older. It's healthy, healthier than getting thin. But my waist is thicker than it used to be."

We look at her waist and then finger our own waists. Some of us frown.

"I don't care for it." Tamara goes on. "But she said it is going to happen, that there is nothing you can do about it.

"Fight it," some one says.

Then we go onto the courts, play hard and high-spirited. Denise and I play two games and quit. Denise passes me on to someone else, someone willing "to get demolished."

After a while I talk with Coach about going to Nationals.

"So have you been playing?"

"No, I've been too busy with final exams at work, exams for the course I'm taking, out-of-town visitors, and all the other things—the dental appointments for this tooth."

"Well, it's good to keep fit."

"I know. I've come in several times late at night, done things in the weight room, but not played."

Coach nods and does up his squash shoes.

"By the way, Coach, one thing about Nationals, I have only one racquet. I need a back-up racquet to take with me, don't you think?"

"Yes, you do. Only one. What kind do you have?"

"Ektelon."

"What number?"

"1200."

"Yes, you need one."

After a pause, I walk away, wishing Coach would volunteer to lend me one of his racquets. As a Teaching Pro he is given many demo racquets and he sells racquets. A decent racquet costs over a hundred bucks. No way do I want to buy another racquet now.

Thinking inventively, I walk up to the women. "Hi everybody, at Nationals, I need a back-up racquet and I don't have one. What should I do?"

Hilary says, "Well, you could borrow mine, but Tamara has it." She grins. "Hum, Tamara."

"No," says Tamara, clutching her Black Knight racquet that is really Hilary's.

"Well," says Hilary, grinning, "I tell you what, you give that one to Joy before I go, and I'll lend you this one while she's gone."

"How many days is it? A weekend?"

"Thursday through Sunday. Four days."

"OK. Sure, no problem. And Hilary, I can use yours?"

"Sure, just let me know, so I remember to leave it here."

"There, you see, now you'll have a racquet, something from us to take with you to Nationals," says Denise.

"Yes," says Hilary, "This is communal, this is support, this is—"

"Sisterhood," I chime in happily, slightly dramatically.

Everyone looks satisfied. We have become a little clutch of women devoted to each other and to our favorite sport. We get good and tired, and then talk about when we might play again. We are busy with vacations, work, yard projects, and out-of-town visitors. In summer, squash doesn't come first.

Hurdles and Hope

My houseguests are due the next day and I worry about one of them getting hurt on the rotten steps of the outside staircase. So I start to repair them—in the poor light of dusk and even though I am tired. Bingo—the hammer slips off a rusty nail and careens against my face. My spectacles catch the blow but do not shatter.

Seeing blood dripping onto my forearms, I stop, look in a mirror, and drive myself to an Emergency Clinic. The damage is a cut on the bridge of my nose between my eyes. The stitches are tiny and will leave only a tiny reddish dot on my skin.

This accident is self-induced, I tell myself. I have made some mistakes: starting the repair when I am tired and not using a trouble light, studying for six hours straight, and ignoring the warnings exuding from my tired self. Is my grief about Rob's departure from the university and relocating to another state welling up in murky ways?

A welcome diversion is the opportunity to host the family I stayed with in Kamloops, British Columbia. On their way to and from the Oregon coast for their holiday the four of them stay with me. They have the pleasure of seeing me with stitches on my nose, but they don't care. Their attention is on what they are seeing on their trip. On impulse I volunteer to guide them to Mount Rainier for some hiking at Paradise, so we spend a day there in its wild flowered majesty.

I am reverently happy about how I am playing and grateful that I am blessed with the ability to play so well at my age. The end of my two years of ups and downs is in sight.

1994 United States National Softball Squash Championships
Meadow Mill Squash Club
Baltimore, Maryland, USA

I am at U.S. Nationals! In a way it feels like a denouement after my two years of preparation. I plan to maximize my experience here.

Twenty-five players from Seattle have flown to Baltimore, mostly from the Seattle Club, only four from the Seattle Athletic Club—three guys, including Coach, and me. I don't know whether Mariza, my fearsome rival, is among the entrants.

I register as a player. While wandering around Meadow Mill Club looking lost and curious, I hear someone ask me, "Are you lost? You look lost."

"Yes, I am. First time at Nationals."

"Just getting the lay of the land, uh?"

"Yes. Thank you."

There are a few organizational quirks, but nothing major. I learn that a shuttle van is running every half hour between the main downtown hotels and the club. I am relieved to discover that Mariza has not entered.

I am on my own, as usual, and unsure of my reception. Although I know the players from my club, I don't expect to hang out with them. The players from the downtown club I don't know well and for the most part, they stick together. Late in the evening one of them, Chris Burrows, informs me that we have missed the final shuttle back to the hotels and, hum, what to do? Get a ride? Take the fast train?

Making quiet noises and showing strong attitude, I say,

1994 United States National Softball Squash Championships

"Let's ask for another shuttle! The loud speakers are bad! We weren't able to hear the announcement that the van was here and ready to depart." Chris takes no initiative on this, so I walk to the registration counter while chirping back to him, "I'll ask for it. I'm a neophyte. I can do anything!"

Chris smiles. I talk with a tournament official and he arranges an extra shuttle bus. Later Chris relates this anecdote to Coach Yusef Khan of the Seattle Club while I am within earshot. People must look for things to talk about in a days-long tournament!

The next day I am standing near Yusef and his entourage and he looks at me in curiosity. "Fifty-Plus?" he asks. "Yes, " I reply steadfastly.

"Good chance, a good chance," he says, while nodding his head up and down.

Chris Burrows says approvingly, "All right! We need to take back a few more trophies—she already got us a shuttle." They smile and disperse.

Yusef probably knows the caliber of play in my age group. Although he hasn't seen me play for over a year, he knows about my number one ranking in British Columbia. He is visibly supportive. Encouragement from him means a lot to me. The Yusef worshippers are right—he does encourage beautifully. I take his attention into myself for myself.

In the first round I am playing Eva Szabo. She is also playing in the "C" draw. I conclude, *"This means she's really a B, playing down for Nationals. I have a chance. If I win the first round, next I meet the #1 seed, Joyce Davenport, and for sure, I lose. Stop! There I go again, predicting what is going to happen on the court, stupid self-defeatist!"*

At the snack bar I get some food. A guy, an older guy,

says hello. We have a pleasant conversation, that is, I listen well, and learn about his family and his line of work. He thinks that some young people who would make good teachers are shying away from teaching because they want more prestige and respect for their expensive university education. They think they are too valuable to work someplace that doesn't appreciate them. This fellow is divorced and I notice him checking my ring-free hands. Ignoring the plea from my friend back home to flirt, I continue to be friendly.

While Yusef Khan and his entourage–including son Azam and daughters Latasha and Shabana–are congregating in the hotel lobby, Shabana greets me. We exchange "When do you play?" questions. Every little exchange with someone who is part of the "in" group makes me feel more comfortable, more like I belong here.

I am curious about the older women around the courts, and wonder who is a player, who an observer. The temptation is to assume that most of the older women here are accompanying their tournament-loving husbands.

Taking some moments at Meadow Mill, I check into matters such as towels, locks, shampoo, hairdryers, practice courts, and lighting. I discover to my satisfaction that most details of this sort have been thought out in a manner that is conducive to high quality play and minimal stress on players.

This tournament experience differs from what I have gotten used to. Doing Canadian tournaments from Seattle has meant driving a long distance by myself, often in the dark and the rain, finding the tournament club in a strange city, playing late at the end of the travel ordeal, finding the home-stay or hostel late at night, lugging everything around

1994 United States National Softball Squash Championships

in my car on Saturday, and then driving home Saturday night or Sunday afternoon, alone, tired and brain-dead. To the conditions of this tournament I can adjust just fine! It is good that I came a day before I am scheduled to compete.

I have not been put in a second event. There are ten players in the Women's 50-55 draw. Champion Joyce Davenport from Pennsylvania is the #1 seed. The #2 seed is Marigold "Goldie" Edwards from Pennsylvania by way of New Zealand. Other players are me from Washington State, Eva Szabo from Pennsylvania, Hazel Jones from Rhode Island, Fiona Goodchild from California, Sandy Vohr from New York, Sharon Schwarze from Pennsylvania, Pat Shulman from New York, and Deming Holleran from New Hampshire

Since I am not scheduled to play until Friday, I slip onto courts in-between matches and hit by myself as well as with some women preparing for a match. I hit on the doubles court, too. No practice court is set aside. I adjust my serve and vision to the wider court.

The rhythm of a competition day includes time spent on cardio-vascular and strength equipment. Copying other players, I do an aerobic rowing workout. Some people—including players—stay courtside a long time and get that glazed-over look in their eyes from too much sitting and watching.

I see some excellent matches, the Pro Men, Men's A, and Women's A. The most memorable match for me is between Goldie Edwards (in her late fifties) and Christina Brownell (late twenties). The veteran wins! Later I see Joyce Davenport play well and win easily.

I take notes on both seeded players, Joyce and Goldie. They were hardball squash champions. They have a completely rounded game plus wisdom and fitness. What dedication!

I introduce myself to Goldie with compliments on her match against Christina. We chat about adding some more Women's age-group categories, such as 55-Plus. The men already have age group 80-Plus.

Drifting here and there, I overhear a few interesting conversations and see a few Pro Men's matches and Women's A matches. The Pro Men do not interest me except from a curiosity viewpoint—like going to the zoo.

I hear some women griping about their low funding for training at the national level. I speculate as to the reasons for this and suspect why they are upset.

The 1994 U. S. Women's National team members are here and I recognize most of them, but being an outsider, I am reticent to engage them. Maybe after my first victory I will feel baptized into this inner hall of competitors. Having time, I stare into faces in the crowd and take in details of this tournament.

I run into Dick and Mary Daly of Seattle. I find out that Mary is a competitive golfer and here to support her husband. (What does it say about me that I have never before bothered to find out a thing about Mary?) For more competitive play Dick is playing down an age group. Last year at Nationals playing in his age group 70-75, he didn't lose a game. This year he is playing in the 65-70 draw.

The squash culture of the youngest players is amazing. The young men are grubby and yacht club cool, practicing the banter and physical greetings that prevail among guys who fit in and know the rules for fitting in. They are high-spirited and happy, showing off with a hair-blowing-in-the-wind camaraderie. They bounce from one action to another. Oddly, I don't come upon groups of young women playing, practicing, or hanging out with each other, though I know some young women are competing here.

Lessons To Learn at a National Tournament:
1. Read the handouts in the registration packet. Learn when and where breakfast is, unless you intend to miss it, as I did my first morning.
2. Organize your clothes, including earrings, the night before, unless you really want to play with earring-free ears. Chances are you are going to dress in the dark so as not to disturb one of your roommates who doesn't have an early match.
3. Take an umbrella. It may rain. There comes a time at a tournament when your system shuts down and refuses to hear another thud of a squash ball. It balks at breathing another breath of stale, ventilated indoor air. Then you have to go outside, regardless of the weather.

The Matches

My first match. I am brilliant.
Strong. Focused. Fast. Merciless.
Scores: 9-0, 9-1, 9-0

Eva isn't very good and I know by watching her hit two warm-up balls that I am better. My playing is almost flawless. I serve one high for a handout and give up one point on a backhand drive tin.

Preparation for my first-ever Nationals match is thorough. Since it is delayed, I have time on my legs. After stretching I swallow a magical potion—1/4 teaspoon of Korean Ginseng Extract (given to me by a Korean student).

Court Quest

Then I do a fast-focus by meditation. Seated outside the quiet doubles court, I zoom into my mind's-eye white spot and angle my body towards the Pacific Northwest. Soon I feel dense warmth emanating from the space between my hands. This combination of being revved up physically and zoomed in mentally is something else! Ta ta!

The referee, Fiona Goodchild, wants to play me. Two younger observers (one scheduled for that court) ask me what category I play in and show a countenance that says, "Where did you come from, I hope we're not in the same draw." When I answer, "50-55 A," the youngsters breathe relief.

I signal myself mentally that with this win, I am baptized into national level squash and truly belong here. I am glad I didn't know one doesn't have to be a high caliber player to enter an age group draw at Nationals. Had I known, I might never have trained so hard!

Coach doesn't see me play. My match was moved to another court, away from the match he was watching, but afterwards I seek him out and he signals me—thumbs up? I signal back the same and finger the score 0-1-0. He mouths, "Whew, shock!"

Soon I get Shabana's eye. In the locker room she had given me some advice: "Keep her back, then drop it—you'll do fine, you hit hard, I've watched you play at our club."

"But that was a couple years ago." I said. To myself I thought, *"That was when I was stronger and slightly out of control."*

"Still," said Shabana, "You're strong, you'll be fine."

Now Shabana asks about my match with eyes and thumbs up. I return the thumbs-up gesture and she registers, "Good."

1994 United States National Softball Squash Championships

My opponent is overwhelmed and mentions how hard I hit. In the middle of our second game, I force myself to discipline my mind because the play is not challenging enough. So as I prepare to serve, I mental my mantra to myself. *"I am one with the ball. I am one with the ball."* When this notion loses intensity, I change to, *"I am the ball. I am the ball."*

Later a nice reward comes in the form of a gentlemanly recognition. The fellow I chatted with my first night here, while touching my shoulder and squeezing my left bicep, says, "You're strong! You played strong."

"Huh, you were watching?"

"Yes," he nods.

"Uh," I say intensely, "It was my first ever Nationals match and I wanted to be focused."

If this fellow has any fantasies about bedding me, he is now having second thoughts. He is an average size fellow and 55-Plus.

The Women's Committee Meeting is packed with energetic, vocal, good-willed, strong, and daring women. The women express predictable growing pains regarding procedural issues, what positions fit our goals, the number of courts at a tournament venue, the number of entrants allowable, and how to configure the draws.

Prize money for the Open-Professional women is a key issue. The women vote to create a separate Women's Open Pro Division with a purse of at least $5000. Zerline Goodman, who makes the motion, gives a public promise to help raise the money. (The Men's Pro Division has a much larger purse and has existed since the 1990-91 season with money donated by a male individual.) Resentment, anger, and disbelief are well controlled within the meeting room.

What do the women sound like in private?

Support for expanding women's squash is evident. There is no debate about the low funding of national team members. There are good ideas for progressive solutions. Camaraderie of common cause is unsquashable.

I speculate again as to why the women's national team funding is inadequate. These outstanding players have to do their own fundraising while they are training. Many of them work or study, too. This is the 1990's after all. It has been twenty years since the second wave of feminism began its surge in North America.

The younger women see the issues from their perspective and do not voice consciousness of recent historical gains in women's squash. The older women bring to the circle their nitty-gritty experiences of building squash for women, weekend by weekend. Women like Carol Weymuller, Hazel Jones and Joyce Davenport speak to historical efforts to develop women's squash. The younger women favor blending protection of women's squash with a daring attitude towards the issues. To the younger ones, boldness and resolute action seem natural.

After the Women's Committee meeting, a group of us walk down to Camden Yard. Prompted by someone's comment that Karen Kelso is looking "Thin 'n trim," I ask her about her training habits. She replies, "Lean is what it means, for moving faster."

To inaugurate myself into national level squash I have worn my favorite outfit. Because the sweating from my first match is not drenching nor long-lasting, I rinse out the top, the skirt, and the headband, and plan to wear the same outfit (with different underwear) the next day for my match against Joyce Davenport (who always wears shorts). My

1994 United States National Softball Squash Championships

roommates do the same thing with their favorite outfits, so the hotel room's steam radiators are strewn with damp skirts and tops.

During the night a capillary pops in my right eye. Does it pop during my nightmare about Killing Fields? *In Viet Nam, Laos, and Cambodia, I am propelling a mature woman over fields of grasses where bodies are decaying, guerrilla soldiers are hiding, land mines exploding, and fear is everywhere. The mature woman looks like my student, a Hmong farmer and appliqué artisan who always appears calm in class.*

During my morning match with Joyce Davenport, I am startled by her serve and precision shots. I know they are coming but can't return them well enough. Joyce expects more from me but doesn't slack off.

Later Joyce says, "During the warm-up you did everything right. You hit high and knew your way around the court. You must have grown up playing on softball courts!"

"No, no," I clarify. "Playing the Vets Circuit last season in British Columbia may have helped, but I started in hardball, like you."

"Yes, hardball." She pauses and smiles. "But in the games, you didn't hit as well."

"Your serve," I defend, "I'm not used to where it hits the wall. It is very precise."

"Uh," she says, "I'm glad, my whole game is based on my serve."

"Well, you saw how I tried to make adjustments to it."

"Uh, yes, you did, and the third game was better."

"Yes."

"It's a privilege to play you, Joyce. For 20 years I've been seeing your name in *Squash News* and wondering, who is she? What is this woman made of?"

Joyce smiles again. "Hard ball days."

"So this last year, for me, finally, everything came together—family, employment, the dates of the tournament, and so on. I said to myself, 'I'm going to do this. I'm going to get there.' "

"You hit well."

Later I ask Joyce if she has ever played Barbara Savage or Jane Cartmel (née Dixon) of British Columbia. "Only in doubles years ago," she says.

"Do you intend to play any more international events soon, for instance, the next Women's Worlds?"

"Don't know," she says. "But then, how many more years am I going to be able to do this? Maybe I will."

Joyce is an athlete in a class by herself. There's a neat respect around her, an easy rapport.

An unusual aspect of our match is the post match refereeing duty. Joyce gets a sub for herself, stands as a line judge, and I learn how to mark the score on an official score sheet.

In the afternoon, I play Pat Shulman and win 9-0, 9-6, 9-2. After observing Pat's relatively slow reflexes during the warm-up, I decide to hard serve her. I am ready— very intense and agile. Afterwards, I sit next to Pat and watch the Women's Open Semi-Final match between Ellie Pierce and Karen Kelso. Ellie wins 3-0. They have phenomenal gets, fitness, court rapport, and many shots that bring "Oohh" from the onlookers.

My evening match against Deming Holleran catches some attention. She is the mother of players Demer and Jennifer Holleran. (Demer is on the U. S. Women's team and is seeded #1 in this tournament.) For our match Deming has her rooting section with her—husband, daughters, friends, and the curious.

1994 United States National Softball Squash Championships

I look around for Coach. Not to be seen. Oh well. I tell myself I don't care if no one is there for me. I am prepared and I will win. Since I got the word from some other players about how Deming plays, and that I should win, I am prepared for her drop and short shots.

Before playing, I take a few moments to sit down and enter into the white light featuring the black ball. The focus is not for long—just until the warmth emanating from my forearms begins to be felt.

Quietly I thank my trainer, Cindy, for teaching me fast lunge-walking as a prelude to play. I do lunges, a few sprints, and jog back and forth near the court as I repeat to myself that I am going to play *safe klean kwik safe klean kwik safe klean kwik*. In fact, my performance plays out as I see it.

During the warm-up, I observe Deming and decide to hard serve while relying on my ability to scramble to short returns. It works. I do almost everything right.

The few times we have a handout, when Deming dribbles a shot to a front corner, her fan group applauds and shouts. Before most serves, while taking a deep breath and spying the black ball, I keep focused and say to myself, *"I am one with the ball, I am one with the ball."*

During the second game the crowd begins to admire my play—and clap for me, too. After the second game, while Momma Holleran is being rushed aside to be coached by her daughters, a fellow stands up and friendly-like reaches toward me and says almost apologetically, "You need your sister here, as coach and fan." He is Deming's husband. I smile in gratefulness for his sensitivity. (Later Deming discloses her family's history in squash. Her husband played squash at university and she watched him and knew if she wanted him, she'd better take it up. Their girls have been competing since they were very young.)

At 3-0 mine (9-1, 9-3, 9-2) there is applause and admiring smiles to me from Deming's crowd and also from the ref to the point where I feel obligated to curtsy, cutely, in response. Later, referee Mary Belknap compliments me. In the locker room there is conversation about where I live, where I have been, and why I haven't played at Nationals before.

Because Sandy Vohr defaults due to the stomach flu, Eva Szabo moves into the Semi-Finals and gets beat by Joyce, so I have to play my first round opponent again! Feed-in Consolations have resulted in this oddity. If I play Eva again and win, I will be the Consolations winner in Women 50-55.

At the tournament desk after my match with Deming, the age thing pops up again. When I question the head referee whether I will have to play Eva again and at what time, he asks me what event and I say, "Women's 50-Plus Consolations."

"You're not 50!" he says, staring at me.

"I'm 51 and-a-half," I say smiling.

He mutters, "I'll be 50."

Oh well, truly I feel nearly invincible against those I played, except for Joyce. She is an elite player, she and her traditional rival, Goldie Edwards. They are among the unsung female athletes who started in the days when it was VERY unusual for women to sweat for a ball.

And me. Li'l old me. Yusef Khan was right and wrong. He was right in that against my non-elite peers I have a "good chance" to take it. But against World and National champions, I don't have a chance, not yet. But somehow losing to them doesn't matter.

Saturday night at the Blue Crab Feast and Dance under

1994 United States National Softball Squash Championships

tents on Pier 500, after wandering and foot burping by myself to the deep beating band music, I am finally pulled into a conversation. It is good, we say, to see more women, especially older women, coming out for sports like squash. We agree that we look better than our non-athletic younger counterparts, and better than same-age men players. We are confident of our healthy bodies. Our bones have been built up densely over the years because of squash, as verified by now popular bone density tests. I mention that my bone densitometry report indicates that at age 50 my bone density exceeded that of the 20-something women in the study. The graying squash players look at me knowingly.

Another aspect of aging comes out in reference to bras. Someone mentions bra cup size and how it gets larger as you get older, even if your weight stays the same. When a college-age player asks why, I explain, "Because your flesh sags out." "Oh," she says, looking puzzled.

Somehow we get into yesterday's play and I assert that I played brilliantly (trying to say it with a tone of complete exaggeration but not succeeding). Goldie smiles and says, "Deming told me she got more points off me than off you." I reply, "I was psyched and I heard Deming would try to drop and I didn't want her to get a run going." Goldie smiles in recognition.

By now I realize that my personality has changed from the me of my first day here— reclusive, disconnected, and quiet to the me of now—bantering, cheerful, and sparkling. A nice smile from Goldie while I am cheerfully chatting with a player tells me she is happy for me, seeing me fitting into the squash scene here.

One more match for me. As usual Goldie and Joyce will play it out for the title in our age group.

Court Quest

My second match against Eva, the Consolation Finals, is a repeat of our first match. Our score is the same: 0, 1, 0. This time Eva's point is not from a tin by me, but from a wristy front corner dribble by her. She tries hard but it is no contest. I hard serve her again and pull off some swift shots. In the warm-up I am a little off, but soon I flow into efficiency. Eva has a three-person crowd cheering and coaching her, but to no avail. After the match we have our picture taken with United States Squash Association President Craig Brand and our trophies. The inscription on my silver bowl reads, "USSRA Rolex Nationals Womens 50+ 5th Place 1994."

After my match I don't have to referee, but I do ref later, a Women's 45-Plus Consolation Final. I have gained confidence using the official score sheet.

After showering, I am free to watch other matches. Zerline Goodman wins over Nancy Cranbury of Canada. Karen Kelso defeats Shabana Khan by default due to illness. In a superb Final Demer Holleran goes five games against Ellie Pierce and wins the Women's Open 1994 Championship.

In other results I note that Chris Burrows and Sue Clinch of the Seattle Club retain their age-group titles. Dick Daly of Seattle wins the old guys draw. In the Men's Open-Pro Division Damian Walker defeats Mark Talbot.

In the Women's 50-Plus Final older Goldie Edwards runs out of breath against Joyce Davenport. Joyce leaves the court in a smiling flurry and accepts congratulations from a bunch of her friends.

I take some photos but run out of film as Joyce and Goldie pose for a photo. During my attempt to photograph the champions, the man who does the write-up for *Squash*

1994 United States National Softball Squash Championships

News comes up to me and asks, "Are you a friend of these women?"

I say, "I played her," pointing to Joyce, "and want to play her," pointing to Goldie.

His voice showing amazement, he says, "These women would crush any man in my club. They are GOOD. I have to write something about each draw for *Squash News*. I'm going to say how good they really are."

"Yes, they're unsung heroic female athletes!"

"Well said!"

Later I see this man passing through the crowd, and his lips tell me, "I've written something really good." We smile at the thought, pleased that we know this secret.

Afterward

The Real Change of Life

It would be untrue to report that I arrived home from Nationals to fanfare and celebration with family and close friends. The women I trained and played with (Tamara, Denise, Leslie, and Hilary) showed only mild interest in how it went. Their responses were mainly questions such as "How was it? How'd you do?" coupled with pleased grins and "Congratulations!" They didn't want to know details. Coach had been there, so he knew how it went and did not need details. My son was back at university doing his thing. My parents and brother and sister weren't interested. Rob was still out of town. As usual, I was on my own. The details of what I went through were reserved for myself to savor.

My goal was to get to U.S. Nationals and play well. I did that. I was satisfied.

Back to my book group I went as promised two years earlier, to celebrate my success with my older women friends. Someone brought a cake with my name on it.

Still not privy to any master plan to change my life, I was astonished when it turned out there was one. Two years later I married that Quaker from Canada and moved to a town in British Columbia that has exquisite wide squash courts.

Glossary

A little of what you need to know to understand this story if you don't play squash:

ALLEY—Unmarked part of a squash court, long skinny area parallel to the sidewalls where you try to get the ball to fly. As in "down the alley," or "down the line."

BOAST—A shot where you make the ball hit the side wall first, then the front wall. There are many kinds of boasts—nick boast, angle boast, reverse angle boast, and trickle boast. Boasts are all fun to try and some are really difficult to do well. Also, if done well, boasts are difficult to return.

BOX, as in **SERVICE BOX**—Red-lined box where you stand when you serve. One box on each side of the court.

CONSOLATIONS—Part of the draw in competition by which a player who loses a match in the first round of play crosses into a secondary draw and plays off for Consolations winner.

CROSSCOURT—A shot where you make the ball travel from one quarter of the court across to the other quarter. It can be hit off your forehand or your backhand.

DROP—A shot where you make the ball drop to the floor after hitting the front wall. A good drop shot requires a good touch so it doesn't bounce out too far.

HANDOUT—When you have served and don't get the point, it's a handout and your opponent gets to serve. You hand the ball over to her. Or, when she has served and she doesn't get the point, the handout is to you.

HARDBALL SQUASH—Type of squash played in parts of North America, mainly the USA, until the 1980's when conversion to the softball game began. The hardball game

Court Quest

features a narrower court, harder ball and scoring to 15 with points won on every serve. Still played in some areas.

LENGTH—As in "good length," or "hit to length," meaning the ball has been hit so that it bounces near the back wall, makes a second bounce, and dies near the back wall. Tough to return well.

LET—A call you make as the incoming striker when you think it's too dangerous to try to hit the ball because your opponent is too close to you or is in standing in the front court where you want to hit the ball. Asking for a "let" means "Let's play the ball again." If you have a referee marking the match, the referee may judge that it's a "No let" situation, and then your opponent gets the point or the hand out. Usually, if you are playing a friendly game with no referee and you ask for a let, your opponent agrees without a fuss.

NICK—A shot that hits the juncture of the floor and the wall, and dies. As in "good nick" because it is impossible to return. Hotshot players can hit nicks at will.

OUT LINE—The area of the court beyond the continuous red line that encloses the court as a playing boundary. If the ball touches the red line at any point—front wall, side walls, or back wall—it is considered "out" and the ball is handed over to your opponent to serve.

If your ball hits beyond the Out Line, you have to hand over the ball to the other player.

RAIL SHOT—A tight-in-the-alley shot that almost grazes the side wall and extends towards the back wall of the court. A power drive hit for length. Easier to do in drills than in a match.

RALLY—A serve or a serve plus a number of returns of the ball, until one player misses. As in "good rally."

Glossary

SCORING—The International or softball version: a game is played until a player gets 9 points, or if it's tied at 8-8 and the person who got to eight first calls for a tiebreaker of one or two points. A player can get a point only when she is serving.

The American or hardball version: play continues to 15 points. If the game is tied at 14-14, the player who got to 14 first has choice of playing one or two play-off points. A player can get a point whether serving or receiving serve.

SERVICE—or Serve. The shot the server uses to get the ball into play. As in Lob Serve.

SERVICE LINE—The red line upon the front wall, extending the full width of the court. A service is not good if the ball is served onto or below this line.

SHORT LINE—The red line that cuts across the middle of the court. If your serve lands in front of this line, it's "short" and you have to give the ball to your opponent.

SOFTBALL SQUASH—Type of squash played in most of the world. The ball is softer than in hardball squash. The court is wider. Scoring is to 9 with points won only by the server.

STROKE—A point or handout awarded to the player who asks for a "let" ball during a rally. The rules for getting a "stroke" rather than a "let" are complex, but basically, if the player was prepared to make a shot that would probably have ended the rally, then a stroke is the fair judgment call. The concept of "stroke" is a source of confusion to squash players.

THE "T"—The area in the center of the court where you try to get after you hit the ball because from there you have the best chance of retrieving the ball your opponent is hitting. It's the place on the court floor where the red lines intersect forming the shape of the letter "T." As in "get back to the T."

TIN—A band of tin 50 centimeters high that runs the entire width of the front court, abutting onto the floor. It makes a distinctive noise when you hit it. If you hit it, you give a point or a handout to your opponent. It's easy to hit the tin, if you don't bend your knees or if the face of your racquet is angled downwards. To "tin it" means the ball is down.

SSRA— Seattle Squash Racquets Association

USSRA— United States Squash Racquets Association

USWSRA—United States Women's Squash Racquets Association

VO2= score, Maximal Oxygen Uptake. I did a bicycle ergometry submaximal exercise test and then my VO2 was predicted by a formula. For a woman age 50-59 a score of 21-25 was poor, 30 or more was excellent. My score was 47-48.

Acknowledgments

Appreciation and thank you go to Trina McKinstry and Robert Stever who read an early version of the manuscript and provided helpful insight and encouragement. Craig Brand, United States Squash Racquets Association, and Barbara Haddleton (née Savage), British Columbia Squash Racquets Association, gave information and encouragement. Brooke Siver, Kamloops squash player, coach and official edited the glossary. Dana Powell-McRann of Kamloops Advanced Sports Physiotherapy clarified information. Andy Beil of Kamloops Macintosh Users Group offered technical support. Librarians at the Kamloops Public Library provided reference help. Mary Lou Routley, University College of the Cariboo instructor and friend, read and edited two drafts of the manuscript. Sandra Larkman Heindsman and Wanda Fullner of Seattle gave editorial advice, guidance, and encouragement. Lynne Stonier-Newman modified the book's title. Graeme Hope came up with the name Bench Press Books. John Schmidt at Canatech.com designed the website for Bench Press Books. Dave Somerville of PixelPerfect created the original cover and logo. Carol Creasy of Little Cottage Graphics did the book's artistic layout and design on her Macintosh with exceptional patience and humour.

Colophon

Research & Communication by Author
Web: Netscape 4.79
Adobe Acrobat 4.05
Power Mac 7500 System 8.1
Color Stylewriter Printer 2400
Writing
Manuscript Preparation: MS-Word 2000

Graphics
Cover Concept and Logo by Dave Somerville using Adobe Photoshop 6 and Adobe Pagemaker 7 on a PC Graphics workstation
Book Design and Layout by Carol Creasy, Little Cottage Graphics
Layout in Quark Express 5.0 on an Apple Macintosh Power Mac G4
Fonts - Adobe Barmeno 14pt and Berkeley Old Style 12pt.
Scanning - Umax Powerlook III
Cover design and interior graphics - Adobe Photoshop 7 on a Mac G4
Proofs- Xerox/Tektronix Phaser 860DP colour laser printer
Book was generated as an Adobe Acrobat PDF file and sent to press via CD in PDF format

Printing
Digital Printing using TR Micropress system by IpoDs, Interior Print on Demand Services
Paper: #24 Premium Bond, 88 Bright
Cover: #65 cover stock, colour laser print from Adobe PDF file, layflat film lamination
Binding: Perfect bound (adhesive, softcover)

Contacts:
info@benchpressbooks.com
ccreasy@jetstream.net
ipods@telus.net

Quick Order Book Form

> ### Court Quest: Playing Women's Squash in the USA and Canada 1992-1994

Phone Orders Toll-Free: 1-800-573-5779
Fax Orders: 1-250-314-6232
Email Orders: info@benchpressbooks.com
Postal Orders: PO Box 453, Kamloops, BC, V2C 5L2, Canada
Website: www.benchpressbooks.com

To order Court Quest: We accept cheque, money order or credit card. If paying by cheque or money order, make payable to Bench Press Books.

In Canada (Canadian funds)   *Quantity*

  Total
Number of books x $20.00 per book
Shipping/handling $2.00 per book

Outside Canada (US funds)
Number of books x $15.00 per book
Shipping/handling $4.00 per book

Shipping Address:

Name_____

Mailing Address_____

_____

City _____ Province/State/Region _____

_____   _____

Thank you for your interest in books from Bench Press Books. We are dedicated to publishing works that large publishers ignore. We would appreciate it, if you told your friends about our efforts.

Bench Press Books